Editor
Janet Cain, M. Ed.

Managing Editor
Ina Massler Levin, M.A.

Editor-in-Chief
Sharon Coan, M.S. Ed.

Illustrator
Sue Fullam

Cover Artist
Barb Lorseyedi

Art Coordinator
Denice Adorno

Imaging
Ralph Olmedo, Jr.
Rosa C. See

Product Manager
Phil Garcia

Publishers
Rachelle Cracchiolo, M.S. Ed.
Mary Dupuy Smith, M.S. Ed.

Year-Round Units for Early Childhood

Author

Jan Burda

Teacher Created Materials, Inc.
6421 Industry Way
Westminster, CA 92683
www.teachercreated.com.

ISBN-0-7439-3100-9

©2001 Teacher Created Materials, Inc.
Reprinted, 2004

Made in U.S.A.

Table of Contents

Table of Contents *(cont.)*

Introduction

Year-Round Units for Early Childhood allows students to experience learning through hands-on activities and the following modalities of learning: visual, auditory, and kinesthetic. Students experience the subjects being taught in new and exciting ways. Lessons focus on getting students involved in a variety of ways and fostering creativity. Thematic teaching is a powerful tool that enhances student learning.

This thematic book includes fun-filled, motivational, field-tested ideas for an entire school year. The lessons and activities are teacher friendly and cover subjects across the curriculum. Each chapter is organized into two themes—usually a science or social studies unit and a holiday unit.

September: Johnny Appleseed and Pets

October: Five Senses and Halloween

November: Native Americans and Thanksgiving

December: Frosty the Snowman and Christmas

January: Sea Life and New Year's Day

February: Valentine's Day and Presidents' Birthdays

March: St. Patrick's Day and Dinosaurs

April: Eggs and Easter

May: Space and Occupations

June: Teddy Bears and Real Bears

Feel free to present the above units in any order that best meets the needs of your students.

Thematic Teaching Across the Curriculum

The monthly themes have been divided into seven unique sections, supporting the units taught in the classroom. Descriptions of the seven sections are given below.

Section 1: Special Day Activities

The 10 Special Days with five center ideas for small group lessons and interactions are prepared on teacher-friendly activity cards. The directions are written in an easy-to-follow format describing materials, time frames, activity sheets, and even extension ideas. All the Special Days include a list of recommended theme-related books and videos, as well as snack suggestions and end-of-the-unit student award certificates.

Section 2: Whole Class Activities

The 10 whole group ideas greatly vary. They include a stuffed animal creative writing lesson, a treasure hunt, and a time for parents to share information about their occupations. These lessons involve the entire class at the same time, without using centers or learning stations.

Section 3: Buddy Time Activities

The 20 bimonthly lessons include directions and activity sheets that are ready to use for cross-age peer tutoring—affectionately called "Buddy Days." Older students pair up with younger students to create and share a variety of learning experiences in subject areas, including art, math, reading, writing, and creative dramatics.

Section 4: Thematic Backpack Buddies

The 10 monthly backpack ideas include a specific buddy (stuffed animal or doll) for each theme, a letter from this buddy, a theme-related book, and a journal writing assignment. Students take turns bringing home each of the thematic backpack buddies.

Section 5: Thematic Art & Poetry Activities

Twenty thematic art ideas, poems, and activity sheets are included in this section. Students' art projects are saved throughout the entire school year. At the end of the year, all the pages are bound into special books.

Section 6: Thematic Pins & Magnets

Every month this section includes six patterns for teachers and two patterns for students to make inexpensive pin or magnet gifts. Simple directions on how to decorate the items help anyone be successful in creating these unique gifts.

Section 7: How to Make a Class Video Book

The 10 complete thematic videotaping ideas include prop suggestions, activity sheet patterns, songs, and poems, plus simple ideas on how to film, edit, and create your own Class Video Book.

How to Use Thematic Teaching Ideas

Section 1: Special Day Activities

Every month, at the culmination of each unit or theme, there is a Special Day. These days include five separate, hands-on activities that are set up at specific centers in the classroom. Divide students into five groups. Have the groups rotate every 20 minutes through the Special Day centers, which include the following kinds of activities: art, science, play area, language arts, and creative dramatics or games.

The dynamics and structure of each Special Day are very important, with each activity taking approximately 20 minutes and allowing five minutes for rotations. Extension ideas are also included for each center. Ideally, you would want to schedule five parent volunteers, teaching assistants, or older students to help run the activity centers. This leaves you free to float from center to center to direct the rotations, help with discipline, and take photographs. This section provides Activity Cards that give detailed descriptions of the center activities. You may wish to laminate the cards and place them in the centers for the volunteers to use. If volunteers are not available to direct the centers, another option is to alternate small groups of students through one center for an entire day. To have students complete all of the activities, set up a different center each day for five days.

At the end of each Special Day, you may wish to give students a theme-related treat. For example, on Dinosaurs' Special Day, students might enjoy eating dinosaur graham cookies. (Be sure to ask parents if their children have any food allergies or dietary restrictions before providing any treats.) If centers are set up for a week, the treats should be passed out on Friday.

In celebration of completing the Special Day and Thematic Unit, you may wish to give students special magnets or pins (Section 6: Thematic Pins & Magnets) and award certificates. The certificates for each unit are included with the Activity Cards.

Section 2: Whole Class Activities

For every month, two themes are listed. One theme has the Special Day activities described above. The other theme has a specific whole group activity that involves the entire class at the same time, without using centers or learning stations. These teacher-friendly ideas often include a recommended theme-related book for you to read aloud and a follow-up activity. These cross-curricular ideas are never the same from month to month. Specific directions for how to prepare and present each lesson are provided.

How to Use Thematic Teaching Ideas *(cont.)*

Section 3: Buddy Time Activities

Before youngsters participate in Buddy Time Activities, you should carefully pair younger students with older students, according to individual needs. For example, active students could be paired with calm, mature students, and high achievers could be paired with low achievers. You and the big buddies' teacher should work together to pair students. The age and developmental level of the buddies are other important factors to consider. It is recommended that the big buddies are at least two to three years older than their little buddies. With this age and maturity difference, there tends to be more nurturing for the younger students and more self-esteem growth for the older students. The activities in this section were created to accommodate these age differences.

It is important that both teachers whose students take part in the Buddy Days prepare their classes for the buddy-time experience. Older students must realize they will be role models for younger students, so it is extremely important that the big buddies set a good example. Younger students need to be reminded that buddy time will be fun, but it is not playtime. Make your behavioral and academic expectations clear to students to ensure that all lessons are completed and everyone in both classes feels safe and successful.

The next step is the bonding time for the buddies. For the first activity of the year, have the big buddies complete, ahead of time, a personal survey that tells about family members, pets, favorite foods, hobbies, etc. When the buddies get together, the big buddies should read their surveys to the little buddies. The little buddies complete their surveys with the help of their big buddies. Then the big and little buddies draw pictures for each other and exchange their surveys.

You may wish to alternate where the Buddy Days take place—one week in the little buddies' classroom, one week in the big buddies' classroom. This helps make both groups of students feel equally important. This also gives the buddies a chance to get to know one another better, take pride in showing and explaining things in their classrooms, and learn more about each other's grade levels.

The Buddy Day lessons vary in content and difficulty and are meant to reinforce many skills for both age groups. Every week try to have the buddies spend 30–45 minutes together. Alternating weeks may be spent reading books, playing outside on the playground, or watching educational videos, such as the *National Geographic* series or *The Magic School Bus*® series, which are appropriate for both age levels.

How to Use Thematic Teaching Ideas *(cont.)*

Section 4: Thematic Backpack Buddies

The backpack buddies are theme-related stuffed animals or dolls. Every day send a backpack buddy home to spend the night with a different student. Place this animal/doll, a thematic book, and a writing journal in a backpack to ensure safe travel to and from school with every student. The journal has blank pages in it, along with a friendly letter from the backpack buddy of the month that explains the student's homework assignment. The following school day, the student returns the backpack and its contents and shares the journal writing assignment with the class.

The backpack buddies may be any inexpensive stuffed creature or doll that matches the description of a character in the thematic storybook.

You may wish to make the writing journals from portfolios with fasteners. Be sure there are enough journal pages for every student in the classroom to complete a writing assignment. Inside each journal place a backpack buddy letter.

Section 5: Thematic Art & Poetry Activities

Each page in this section represents a monthly unit and includes a special thematic poem, directions and activity sheets for a specific art project, and a student interview sheet on which children record their favorite school memories. In addition, there is a place for an optional monthly student photograph.

Save the completed student art projects. Mount each on a piece of colored construction paper. You may wish to enlist the help of parent volunteers or teaching assistants for this task. Every monthly activity has a suggested layout for displaying the artwork, poem, photograph, and interview. File and save each student's completed pages in a portfolio. Keep the pages in the order that the units were taught. At the end of the year, make books by binding each student's pages together.

Students decorate the front cover of their books with painted handprints and a large photograph of themselves. You may wish to display the Thematic Art & Poetry Books on students' desks for an Open House or a similar type of event. Then encourage students to take home and keep their books as colorful reminders of the fun-filled learning experiences the class had throughout the school year.

How to Use Thematic Teaching Ideas *(cont.)*

Section 6: Thematic Pins & Magnets

Make these inexpensive thematic pins and magnets for holiday gifts or special rewards at the end of a monthly unit. You may also wish to give students award certificates after a Special Day (Section 1). Small and large patterns for the thematic pins and magnets are provided. The large patterns will be easier for young children to use.

The materials needed for creating these unique gifts include:

1. vinyl, stiff felt, or tagboard

2. fabric and craft paint pens, glitter glue, fine-point permanent markers, or embroidery paint

3. white all-purpose glue or tacky glue

4. small plastic eyes (optional)

5. pins and/or business card magnets

Craft stores or yardage shops carry most of the items listed above. Office supply stores usually sell business card magnets, which are very thin self-stick magnets that can easily be cut into strips using scissors. Place the magnetic strips or pins on the back of your completed patterns. Remember, the larger the cut-out pattern, the larger the magnetic strip or pin will need to be.

Depending on whether you use vinyl, stiff felt, or tagboard, the price will differ. Vinyl is the most durable and by far the least expensive. It can be purchased in a variety of colors, thicknesses, and textures. It takes only one-eighth of a yard (91 cm) that has a width of 55 inches (140 cm) to make 30 or more small gift pins or magnets. As a result, it is possible to make 30–35 pins or magnets for an inexpensive price.

Additional decorating suggestions accompany the different gift patterns. This is a time for fun and creativity!

How to Use Thematic Teaching Ideas *(cont.)*

Section 7: How to Make a Class Video Book

The Class Video Book production actually takes very little preparation time and only basic knowledge of videotaping. It is helpful to have a parent volunteer or another teacher do the videotaping each month so that you can be free to direct and help discipline students.

Songs, poems, interviews, and a list of videotaping props are provided for each monthly taping session. At the end of the year, the entire tape is usually 90 minutes long.

The Class Video Book requires very little editing. In fact, the video shop that reproduces the tape should be able to do any editing that is needed. The cost of this priceless memory for students and parents is very reasonable. You may wish to give parents the option of taking a copy of this video home and reproducing it themselves. Consider playing a copy of the tape during an Open House or a similar type of event for all to view and enjoy.

Listed below are some general suggestions for filming the Class Video Book.

1. Leave five minutes of blank time at the beginning of the tape so that a title and students' names can be inserted at a later time.
2. If possible, place the video camera on a tripod. This relieves the camera operator of having to hold the camera the entire time.
3. Keep it simple. Do not do any editing until the very end of all the segments.
4. Each monthly taping should be only 10–15 minutes in length.
5. Videotape at the culmination of each unit so students know the poems and songs to recite and sing.
6. After each filming session, make a copy of the master tape. This will serve as a backup in case anything happens to the original.
7. Use the same camera operator and camera for all the segments filmed.
8. Use only one videocassette (approximately 90 minutes) for the master tape. Simply add segments to it by videotaping each month. Each unit provides specific videotaping directions for each thematic unit, as well as patterns for props, words for songs, etc. Be sure to place a videotape label on the tape itself, listing important information about the Class Video Book.

Below is an example of what an individual child's video label might look like.

Class Video Book for the _____ School Year

_____ 's Special Memory

Grade Level: _____   Teacher: _____

Note: The child's name goes in the second blank.

September Themes:
Johnny Appleseed and Pets

Section Contents

Bibliography

Hopkins, T. *1001 Best Web Sites for Educators*. Teacher Created Materials, 2000. URL updates are available at the following address: *http://www.teachercreated.com*

Johnny Appleseed

Greene, Carol. *John Chapman: The Man Who Was Johnny Appleseed*. Grolier Publishing, 1996.

Hall, Zoe. *The Apple Pie Tree*. Scholastic, 1996.

Kellogg, Steven. *Johnny Appleseed: A Tall Tale*. William Morrow, 1988.

Silverstein, Shel. *The Giving Tree*. HarperCollins Children's Books, 1986.

Tall Tales and Legends: Johnny Appleseed. Videotape. Lyrics Studios, 1995. 50 minutes.

Pets

Brett, Jan. *The First Dog*. Harcourt Brace Jovanovich, 1988.

Let's Explore—Furry, Fishy, Feathery Friends. Videotape. Tapeworm, 1995. 30 minutes.

Pilkey, Dav. *Dogzilla*. Harcourt Brace, 1993.

Pilkey, Dav. *Kat Kong*. Harcourt Brace, 1993.

Urquhart, Jennifer. *The Pets You Love*. National Geographic Society, 1991.

Weller, Frances Ward. *Riptide*. The Putnam Publishing Group, 1996.

Activity Card #1

Activity Card #1: Apple Mobiles
Supplies:
- 6" x 6" (15 cm x 15 cm) red construction paper squares, one per student
- 1" x 2" (2.5 cm x 5 cm) green rectangle, one per student
- hole puncher
- yarn or string, one piece per student
- "My Apple Tree" poem and Apple with a Bookworm, one per student and one for the center (page 18)
- scissors
- glue
- crayons or markers
- white drawing paper, one piece per student (optional)

Instructions:
1. Distribute the copies of the poem "My Apple Tree" to students at the center.
2. Read the poem to them.
3. Tell students that you are going to reread the poem, leaving out the rhyming words. Ask them to say the missing rhyming words as you read the poem the second time.
4. Reread the poem, allowing students to fill in the rhyming words.
5. Ask students to cut out the poem.
6. Give each student a red square and a green rectangle. Tell students that the red square represents an apple and the green rectangle represents a stem.
7. Have students glue the apple poem onto the red squares.
8. Then tell youngsters to glue the green stem onto the top of the red square.
9. Demonstrate how to turn a square into a circle by cutting off the corners.
10. Have students cut off the four corners of their square. Provide assistance to any student who needs it.
11. Have students draw a face on the blank side of the apple and write their names on the stem.
12. Punch a hole at the top of each stem.
13. Tie a piece of yarn or string through the hole in each apple stem.
14. Hang the mobile from the ceiling or a light fixture.

Extension: Provide white drawing paper for students to copy the Apple with a Bookworm picture (page 18). Help students read the joke.

Activity Card #2

Activity Card #2: Star Story and Star Prints

Supplies:

- large white construction paper, one or more pieces per student
- red water-based paint
- five Styrofoam or plastic bowls
- five apples
- sharp knife (for adult use only)
- "Solar's Wish," one per student and one for center (pages 19 and 20)
- Parts of an Apple, one per student (page 21, optional)

Instructions:

1. Before any students come to the center, cut the five apples in half across the middle as shown in the illustration. Set aside half of one apple to show each center group the star shape in the middle.

2. When a group of students arrive at the center, distribute copies of the story "Solar's Wish."

3. Read the story aloud to students.

4. After reading the story, say, *Now, children, would you like to see what Solar looks like?*

5. Show students the inside of the apple you have set aside. Point out the star pattern in the middle. Remember to set this half of an apple aside for the next group.

6. Pour red paint into the bowls. Show students how to dip half of an apple into the red paint and make star prints on a piece of white paper. Tell students not to use too much paint so that the star can easily be seen in the print.

7. Give students the white construction paper.

8. Allow youngsters to make star prints on their papers. Encourage students to fill their papers with star prints.

Extension: Distribute copies of the Parts of an Apple diagram. Discuss the diagram. Invite students to color the apple.

Activity Card #3

Activity Card #3: Apple Class Book

Supplies:

- large white board, a chalkboard, or a large piece of butcher paper; one per group
- Apple Class Book, one per student (page 22)
- crayons or markers
- pencils
- slices from different kinds of apples (red delicious, golden delicious, pippin, gala, Granny Smith, etc.)

Instructions:

1. Ask students to brainstorm a list of different foods made from apples. (Examples: apple pie, applesauce, candied apples, apple dumplings)

2. Write students' suggestions on the white board, chalkboard, or piece of butcher paper.

3. Distribute the Apple Class Book activity sheet to students at the center.

4. Ask children to draw two or three foods made from apples.

5. In the blank at the bottom of the page, have students write names of the apple foods they have drawn. Depending on your students' skill level, you may wish to have youngsters dictate the words for you to write.

6. After all students have been to this center, staple the activity pages together to make a class book.

7. You may wish to make an apple star print picture for the cover.

WARNING: Be sure to ask parents if their children have any food allergies or dietary restrictions before allowing students to taste the apples for the Extension activity.

Extension: Teach students the names of the different kinds of apples you have sliced. Allow youngsters to sample the different kinds of apples. Ask children to compare and contrast the taste of the different kinds of apples.

Activity Card #4

Activity Card #4: Johnny Appleseed Poem and Paper Doll

Supplies:

- light blue construction paper, one piece per student
- Johnny Appleseed Poem and Paper Doll, one per student (page 23)
- scissors
- glue
- crayons

Instructions:

1. Explain the legend of Johnny Appleseed.

   The legend of Johnny Appleseed is based on a real pioneer named John Chapman. This man traveled across the wilderness, making friends with pioneers, Native Americans, and forest animals. Johnny was a gentle, kind person who planted apple seeds wherever he went. As a result of his planting so many apple seeds, his nickname became Johnny Appleseed.

2. Give each student a large piece of blue construction paper and a Johnny Appleseed Poem and Paper Doll page.

3. Read aloud the poem to students.

4. Invite students to color and cut out the paper doll.

5. Have students glue the paper doll onto the construction paper.

6. Encourage students to draw apple trees, forest animals, and Native American and pioneer friends around the Johnny Appleseed paper doll.

7. Then tell students to cut out the poem and glue it onto the back of the construction paper.

Extension: Obtain different versions of the Johnny Appleseed story and books about apples and apple trees for students to look at and read.

Activity Cards #5

Activity Card #5: Counting Apples Game

Supplies:

- tan or brown construction paper, one piece per student
- white construction paper, one piece per student
- number cubes; one per younger student, two per older student
- scissors
- pencils
- glue
- crayons or markers

Instructions:

1. Distribute the tan or brown construction paper to students.

2. Have each student lay one arm and hand flat on the tan or brown construction paper. Tell them to hold that arm and hand still while they trace around it. Explain that their arms will make apple tree trunks and their hands will make the branches. Help younger students as needed.

3. Have students cut out the tree patterns they have made by tracing their arms and hands.

4. Give each student a piece of white construction paper.

5. Tell youngsters to glue the tree patterns onto the white construction paper.

6. Ask students to use a green crayon to color grass at the base of the tree and leaves on the tree branches.

7. Show students how to roll a number cube and read the number that is at the top of the cube when it stops rolling. If you are playing with older students, show them how to read and add the numbers that are at the tops of the cubes.

8. Have students take turns rolling the number cube.

9. Tell students that whatever number they roll on the number cube is the number of apples they should draw on their apple trees.

10. Allow time for students to color the apples on their trees.

11. After students are done coloring their apples, count with children to determine the total number of apples that they have colored as a group.

12. Tell students to record the total number of apples on the back of their papers.

Extension: Five small apples and five large spoons are used for apple races. Have students balance the apples in their spoons and run or walk fast to cross the finish line and win.

Award Certificate

Give students the Johnny Appleseed's Special Day Award Certificates after they have completed all five center activities. You may prefer to fill in individual student names ahead of time.

✂ -

Congratulations to _____

for completing the

Johnny Appleseed's Special Day Centers!

_____   _____
          Teacher   Date

✂ -

Congratulations to _____

for completing the

Johnny Appleseed's Special Day Centers!

_____   _____
          Teacher   Date

Apple Poem

My Apple Tree

Walking by my apple tree,

A branch gently tickled me.

Then I was lifted oh, so high,

A little bird flew right by.

Up there I found a tasty treat—

A giant apple I could eat!

I picked the apple, juicy and round.

My tree smiled and put me down.

Apple with a Bookworm

Joke: What is worse than finding a whole worm in your apple?

Answer: Finding half a worm.

Solar's Wish

Once there was a bright star that twinkled high in the night sky above planet Earth. He was a young star named Solar. This star had the heart of an explorer. Every night as he stared and winked, the most beautiful planet in his solar system would come into view. Solar secretly wished he could visit and explore this planet. Soon it was all little Solar could think about. To make his wish come true was not going to be easy. He would have to receive permission from Earth's mother star, called the Sun.

One night Solar built up his courage and whispered his request to the Sun. Many other stars had asked the Sun for permission to do things, but nothing was as unusual as Solar's request. The Sun knew Solar was sincere about his request, so after a thoughtful period of 24 hours, the Sun finally told Solar he could go to Earth. However, there was one important rule this young star had to follow. The Sun told Solar that he must use a disguise so the human species on Earth would not know he was a celestial light, or star. Solar immediately agreed.

Quick as a twinkle, the Sun's magic and Earth's gravity pulled young Solar right out of the night sky. Splash! Solar landed headfirst in one of Earth's oceans. "Brrrr!" said Solar. Solar instantly changed himself into a starfish. At first this disguise seemed to work well. But by morning Solar was stuck in a tide pool. Children of the human species found him and picked him up. The children played with Solar's arms and tickled his tummy. Solar thought, "Oh, no! This will never do!"

So, quick as a twinkle, Solar changed himself into a white star on an American flag. He was high up on a flagpole. Almost every morning a group of children would salute him. This was fun for a week or two, but then Solar longed to see other parts of the planet Earth.

Quick as a twinkle, Solar changed himself again. This time he became a Christmas tree star. He sat on top of the most beautiful mountain pine tree in a lush green forest. Solar rested there for many months enjoying the beautiful scenery all around him.

One winter day, a human family climbed that mountain. The human boy saw Solar on top of the pine tree and yelled, "Mom! Dad! That's the Christmas tree I want. Look! It already has a star on top!" So the human family chopped down Solar's pine tree. Solar and his tree were carried down the mountain and put inside a human habitat called a house. "Oh, no!" thought Solar. The young star knew he was in trouble again and that he would have to find a way to escape as soon as possible.

Solar's Wish *(cont.)*

After the human family went to sleep that night, Solar started thinking about where he should go hide this time. That was when he heard a soft whisper coming from outside the house. At first Solar thought it was just the wind saying his name. But then there was a gentle tapping on the window. Solar looked up and saw an old apple tree smiling at him through the glass pane. Her branches were doing the tapping to get his attention.

The cracked mouth on the old apple tree's trunk started to speak. In a whisper she said, "Come, little star. Come and use me for your next hiding place. No one will find you, and we will become great friends. I've been on Earth for over 145 years now, and I can tell you a lot of its secrets."

"I guess I have nowhere else to go," said Solar. "But where will I hide without being seen by the human species?" Solar asked the old apple tree.

It was then that the wise old apple tree pointed with one of her branches to a beautiful red apple. "Jump inside one of my apples," she said. "It will be cozy and safe. Don't be afraid, Solar."

Solar built up his courage and after a slooooow twinkle, he slipped into one of the old tree's red apples. And guess what? It was cozy. It was safe. And the apple tree and Solar did become great friends.

To this day, Solar still lives inside the apple—silently listening to us, watching us, and learning all about this beautiful blue planet called Earth. In fact, many of Solar's buddy stars have now joined him. They hide inside apples around the world, enjoying their cozy hiding places while making friends with their special protectors, the apple trees.

Parts of an Apple

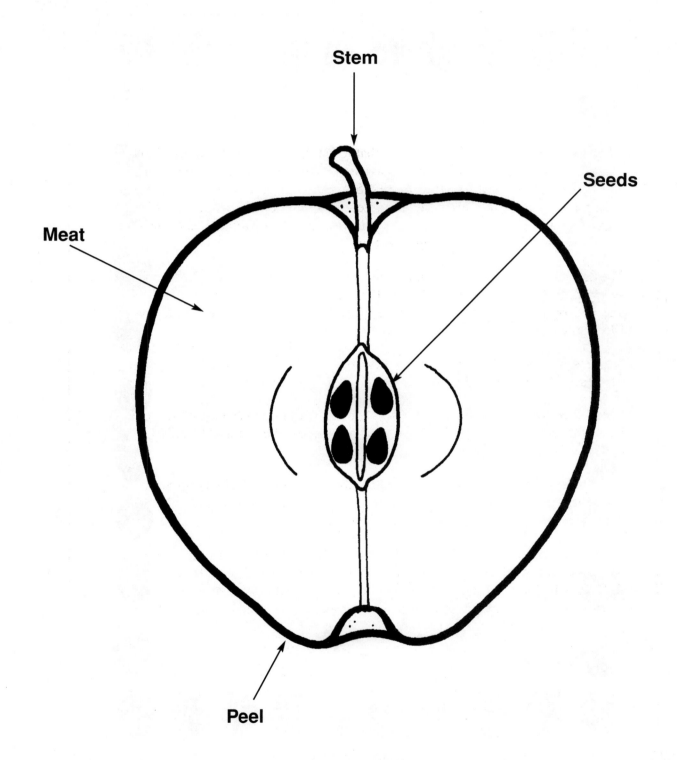

Apple Class Book

Name: _____ Date: _____

Here are some special foods made from apples: _____

_____.

Johnny Appleseed Poem and Paper Doll

Johnny Appleseed

Johnny Appleseed loved apple trees.

He spent his life planting those seeds.

Everywhere Johnny went

An apple tree he did plant.

He made friends across the land

By always giving a helping hand.

Color and cut out the Johnny Appleseed paper doll.

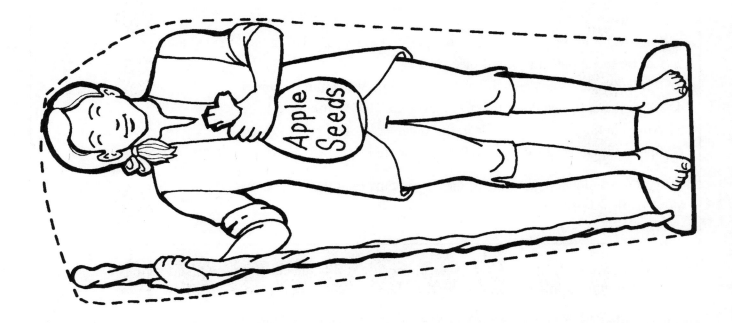

Snack Ideas and Recommended Book

Supplies:

- ingredients for Chunky Applesauce Recipe (listed below)
- plastic knives
- pot and stove, slow cooker, or crock pot
- masher
- large spoon

- small cups, two per student
- plastic spoons, one per student
- graham crackers, one per student
- apple juice

WARNING: Be sure to ask parents if their children have any food allergies or dietary restrictions.

Instructions:

After completion of all five centers, invite students to enjoy a snack of applesauce, graham crackers, and apple juice. You may wish to have students help make the simple applesauce recipe shown below by using the plastic knives to cut up two apples each. This recipe makes enough for five students. Depending on the number of students participating, increase the amount of the ingredients.

Chunky Applesauce Recipe

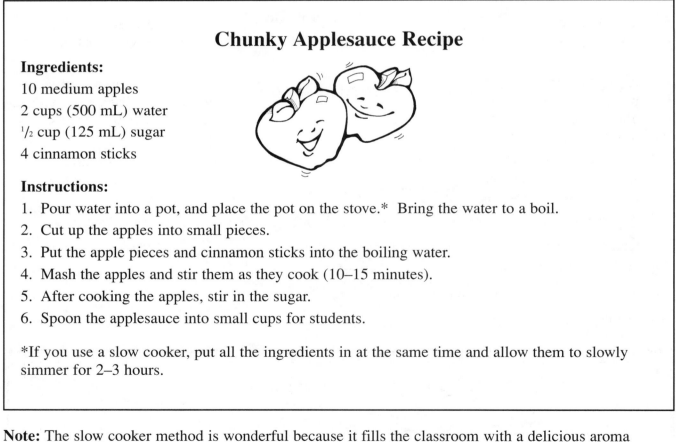

Ingredients:

10 medium apples

2 cups (500 mL) water

¹/₂ cup (125 mL) sugar

4 cinnamon sticks

Instructions:

1. Pour water into a pot, and place the pot on the stove.* Bring the water to a boil.
2. Cut up the apples into small pieces.
3. Put the apple pieces and cinnamon sticks into the boiling water.
4. Mash the apples and stir them as they cook (10–15 minutes).
5. After cooking the apples, stir in the sugar.
6. Spoon the applesauce into small cups for students.

*If you use a slow cooker, put all the ingredients in at the same time and allow them to slowly simmer for 2–3 hours.

Note: The slow cooker method is wonderful because it fills the classroom with a delicious aroma throughout Johnny Appleseed's Special Day.

Recommended Book: On Johnny Appleseed's Special Day, read aloud *Johnny Appleseed: A Tall Tale*, retold and illustrated by Steven Kellogg (William Morrow, 1988).

Pets Whole Class Activity

Supplies:

- *Riptide* by Frances Ward Weller (The Putnam Publishing Group, 1996)
- large piece of butcher paper
- My Favorite Pet, one per student (page 26)
- markers or crayons
- pencils
- glue
- large letters for the title *Our Best Friends*
- magazines (optional)
- scissors (optional)
- photograph of each student (optional)

Instructions:

1. Read aloud the book *Riptide*. This book is an incredible true story about a golden retriever dog named Rip for short. He saves a little girl from drowning and becomes a real-life hero with the honorary title of being the nineteenth lifeguard on Nauset Beach.

2. Discuss the story with students.

3. Ask students to brainstorm other ways pets help people. Possible answers: by giving us love, by talking and listening to us, by watching over us and protecting us, by entertaining us, by calming us down, by playing with us, by being our best friends.

4. Distribute the copies of My Favorite Pet to students. Tell children to draw themselves with their favorite pets. Tell students that the "favorite pet" may be any pet they have ever owned or a pet that belongs to someone else.

   As an alternative to having students draw pictures, you may prefer to allow children to cut out photographs of real pets or magazine pictures of pets they would like to own. Then have students glue the pictures onto the activity sheet. After the glue dries, ask youngsters to draw themselves next to the pet picture.

5. Tell students to complete the sentences at the bottom of the activity sheet, using inventive spelling. Depending on the skill level of your students, you may prefer to allow children to dictate their responses for you to write on their activity sheets.

6. After students have finished the activity, invite them to share their pictures and responses.

7. Collect the papers, and cut around each page in free-form style.

8. Glue the title *Our Best Friends* at the top of the butcher paper.

9. Then create a mural by mounting the activity sheets on the butcher paper.

10. Display the mural on a bulletin board or classroom wall.

Our Best Friends

My Favorite Pet

Name: _____ Date: _____

Draw a picture of you with your favorite pet.

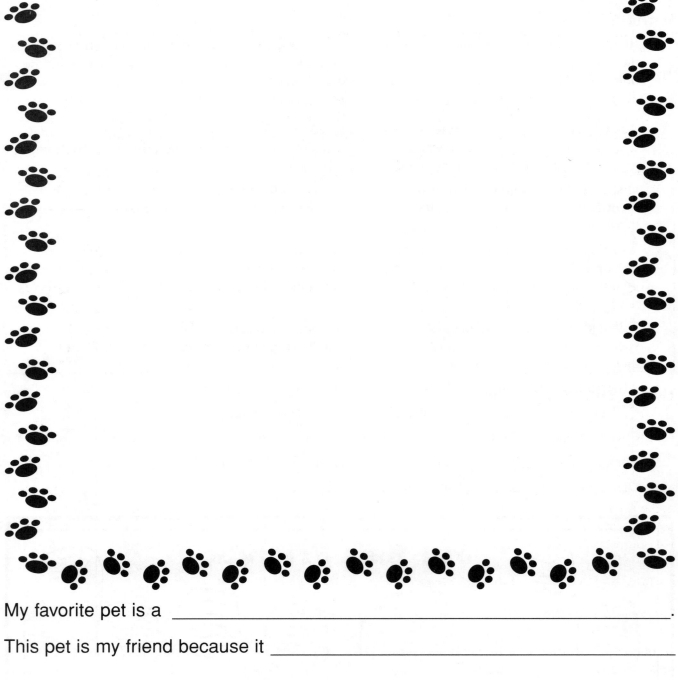

My favorite pet is a _____.

This pet is my friend because it _____

_____.

Buddy Time Activities

Buddy Interviews

Reproduce the Buddy Time Interview form (page 28). Make enough copies for each big and little buddy to have one. If possible, make the copies for the little buddies a different color than the copies for the big buddies. Ask the big buddies to fill out their interview forms first. Then invite them to bring their forms to the little buddies' classroom. Tell the big buddies to read and discuss their interview forms with their little buddies. Then allow time for the little buddies to complete their forms with the help of their big buddies. Tell the big and little buddies to exchange their interview forms. Encourage the buddies to keep each other's forms so they will get to know one another better. This is a wonderful activity to do at the beginning of the year. It helps the buddies feel more comfortable with one another by setting the stage for many special bonding moments throughout the upcoming months.

Buddy Self-Portraits

Reproduce the Our Self-Portraits activity sheet (page 30), one per big and little buddy. Distribute the activity sheets, and explain what a self-portrait is. On the chalkboard, demonstrate how to draw a simple person, using the steps shown below. Tell the big and little buddies to use a pencil to draw a self-portrait. Then have the buddies use crayons to color the eyes, hair, clothes, and shoes on their self-portraits. You may wish to take a photograph of the big and little buddies to glue onto their self-portraits. Display the self-portraits on a classroom wall or bulletin board.

Buddy Time Stuffed Pet Story

Reproduce the Buddy Time Stuffed Pet Story (page 29), one per big and little buddy. Ahead of time, send a note home to the little buddies' parents asking them to send a small or medium-sized stuffed animal to school with their children on the date that you plan to do this activity. Have a few extra stuffed animals on hand for youngsters who forget to bring theirs. To begin this lesson, distribute the copies of the Buddy Time Stuffed Pet Story to students. Have the big buddies help the little buddies make up a story about the stuffed pet by filling in the blanks on the Buddy Time Stuffed Pet Story activity sheet. On the back of the story, have the big and little buddies draw and color the stuffed pet. If you prefer to have children make a larger picture of the stuffed pets, provide each pair of buddies with a piece of large white construction paper. Staple the stories to the pieces of construction paper. Display students' work in the classroom.

Extension: Here are a few extension ideas. Have the big and little buddies use tape measures to take measurements of the stuffed pets' arms, legs, waist, etc. Provide a balance scale and one-inch (2.5 cm) wooden cubes for buddies to weigh the stuffed pets. Have the buddies design homes for the stuffed pets using cardboard boxes, paper bags, or milk cartons, depending on the size of the stuffed pet. Remind students to make air holes in the homes they design.

Buddy Time Interview

Complete the Buddy Time Interview. Fill in as many blanks as possible.

My name is _____ .

My buddy's name is _____ .

My favorite thing to do at school is _____ .

There are _____ people in my family.

The names of the people in my family are _____

_____ .

I have a pet named _____ . It is a _____ .

My favorite food is _____ .

My favorite television show is _____ .

My favorite cartoon is _____ .

If I could go anywhere for a vacation, I would like to go to _____ .

My favorite type of candy is _____ .

My favorite color is _____ .

My favorite sport or game is _____ .

My favorite number is _____ .

Someday I would like to be a _____ because

_____ .

Something I'm afraid of is _____ .

Sometimes I'm really happy when _____ .

I'm sad when _____ .

Something I do very well is _____ .

Something I have a hard time doing is _____

_____ .

28

Buddy Time Stuffed Pet Story

Little Buddy's Name: _____

Big Buddy's Name: _____

Complete the Stuffed Pet Story by filling in the blanks.

My stuffed pet's name is _____ .

The type of animal it is is a _____ .

One day my stuffed pet came alive and said, " _____."

I took my stuffed pet to a special place called _____ .

When we got there, we were both so hungry that we ate _____ .

Then I introduced my stuffed pet to two special friends. My friends' names

are _____ and _____ . Next I made my

stuffed pet a house out of _____ . My stuffed pet got

thirsty, so I gave it some _____ to drink. Then my

stuffed pet wanted to go for a ride in my _____ .

We went very fast! After our ride, my stuffed pet fell asleep in my lap. At the

end of the day, I took my stuffed pet home.

Draw a picture of your stuffed pet on the back of this paper or on a piece of construction paper.

Our Self-Portraits

Little Buddy's Name: _____

Big Buddy's Name: _____

My Big Buddy and Me

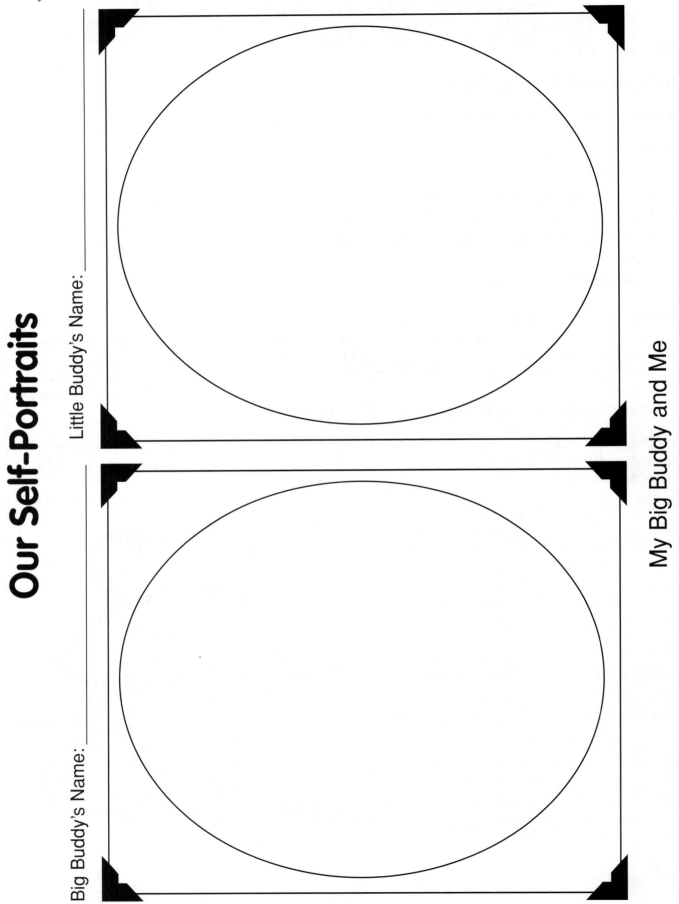

Mouse Backpack Buddy

September Theme: Pets

Backpack Buddy: small stuffed mouse

Storybook: *Dogzilla* by Dav Pilkey (Harcourt Brace, 1993)

Supplies:
- journal
- Letter from Mouse Backpack Buddy (page 32)
- Journal Assignment, one per student (page 33)
- white construction paper, one piece per student
- backpack
- Mouse Backpack Buddy

Instructions:

You may wish to make the writing journals from portfolios with fasteners. Be sure there are enough journal pages (copies of page 33) for every student in the classroom to complete the writing assignment. Also place a copy of the Letter from Mouse Backpack Buddy inside the journal. The homework assignment is described for parents and students in this letter. However, you may prefer to explain the assignment to students before they take it home.

For this journal assignment, students read the book *Dogzilla*, make a pet collage out of magazine and newspaper pictures or personal drawings, and write some ideas for new and humane ways to rid the town "Mousopolis" of some strange creatures called "puppies."

Before sending the backpack home with a different child each day, check to be sure it has the small stuffed mouse, the book *Dogzilla*, the writing journal, and a blank piece of white construction paper inside. Remind the student who is taking these materials home to return the backpack and its contents the next school day. When it is the next school day, allow time for the student who took the backpack home to share his/her collage and journal writing assignment with the class.

Be sure every student has an opportunity to take the backpack home. After all students have completed the writing assignment, make the journal a permanent addition to your classroom library. You may wish to display students' collages.

Letter from Mouse Backpack Buddy

Squeak! Squeak! Squeak!

I'm Squeaky, one of the mice from Dav Pilkey's book *Dogzilla*. I live with my fellow mice in the quiet little mouse city called Mousopolis. We had a major problem last summer during our first annual barbecue cook-off. Our problem's name in the book is Dogzilla. After you and your parents read the storybook that is in the backpack, you'll understand how scary Dogzilla was to little mice like us. Well, my friends and I outsmarted that creature, but you'll have to read the story to find out how!

This year we have a new problem with some creatures called puppies. They smell and look a lot like Dogzilla, but they are smaller. Unfortunately their size does not make a difference because there are four of them. Help! The other mice and I have our work cut out for us once again. Our goal is to rid Mousopolis once and for all of these dreadful, messy creatures called puppies.

Maybe you can help us. After you read *Dogzilla*, please use a page in this journal to write down any kind and humane ways you can think of for getting rid of these puppies from our peaceful city. All suggestions are welcome!

After you finish the journal writing assignment, you and your parents should use the white construction paper to make an animal collage. First cut out animal pictures that you find in magazines and newspapers or that you have drawn by yourself. Then glue the pictures onto the construction paper. Let the glue dry before you put your collage in the backpack.

Tomorrow, please put the book *Dogzilla*, this journal, your collage, and me inside the backpack and return all of these things to your teacher. You will get to share your collage and ideas with the class, and another student will get to take me home.

Thanks so much for your help.

Sincerely,

Squeaky

Journal Assignment

Dear Squeaky,

Here are some kind and humane ways to rid your city of those creatures called puppies.

_____

_____

_____

_____

_____

_____

_____

_____

_____

_____

_____

_____

Sincerely,

_____

Art & Poetry Activities

Apple Tree

Supplies:

- large yellow construction paper, one piece per student
- round dime-size sponges, one per student
- crayons
- glue
- red water-based paint
- plastic or Styrofoam bowls, one for every two students
- "Apple Tree" poem, kite pattern, and "September" title; one per student (page 35)
- Favorite Memories, one per student (page 37)

Instructions:

Give each pair of students two sponges and a bowl of paint. Give students the yellow construction paper. Help them fold the papers in half so they open like a book. On one-half of the paper, have each child color a brown tree trunk and green leafy branches. Show children how to dip a sponge in paint to make a print. Invite students to make sponge-print apples in their trees. Distribute the top part of page 35. Tell youngsters to color and cut out the kite patterns. Have them glue the kites onto the apple tree branches. Students may wish to add a face and tail to the kites. Read the poem "Apple Tree" to students. Ask children to cut out the poems and glue them onto the blank halves of their papers. Then have students cut out the "September" titles and glue them on the construction paper. Distribute the Favorite Memories activity sheets, and help students complete them. Then have students glue them onto the backs of the construction paper.

Little Fish

Supplies:

- large green construction paper 12" x 18" (30 cm x 46 cm), one piece per student
- "Little Fish" poem and fish pattern, one per student (page 35)
- Fish Bowl Pattern, one per student (page 36)
- crayons
- glue
- blue watercolor paint
- paintbrushes, one per student
- plastic or Styrofoam bowls, one for every two students
- Favorite Memories, one per student (page 37)

Instructions:

Distribute the bottom part of page 35 and the Fish Bowl Pattern. Have students color the fish pattern, cut it out, and glue it in the fish bowl. Encourage students to color plants, pebbles, air bubbles, and smaller fish in the fish bowl. Give each pair of students two paintbrushes and a bowl with blue paint. Have children paint blue watercolor over the entire fish bowl. Allow the paint to dry. Distribute the construction paper. Help students fold it in half so it opens like a book. Read the "Little Fish" poem to students. Have them cut out the poem. Ask them to glue the poem on one-half of the construction paper and the fish bowl on the other half. Then have students cut out the "September" title and glue it on the construction paper. If students have not already done a Favorite Memories activity sheet, help them complete one now. Tell them to glue it onto the back of this artwork.

September Poems

Apple Tree

Apple tree with branches so high,

You grabbed my kite as it flew by.

Won't you give it back to me?

I'll post a sign saying, "Be kind to this tree!"

I'll water your roots and read to you;

I'll pick up your leaves and apples, too.

So while the sun shines and it's still light,

Won't you, please, let go of my kite?

September

Kite Pattern

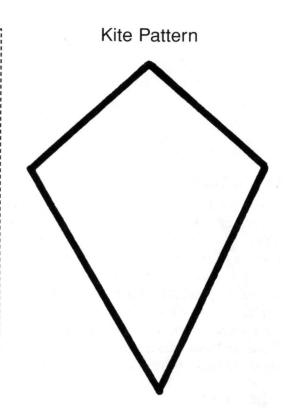

Little Fish

Little fish I won at the fair,

Why do you like to swim and stare?

Little fish, floating by,

Do you ever want to fly?

Little fish, stuck in your dish,

Would you like to make a wish?

September

Fish Pattern

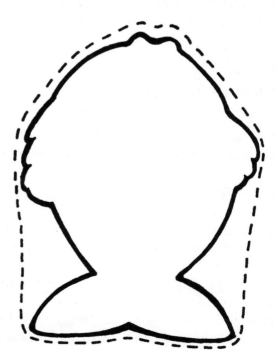

Fish Bowl Pattern

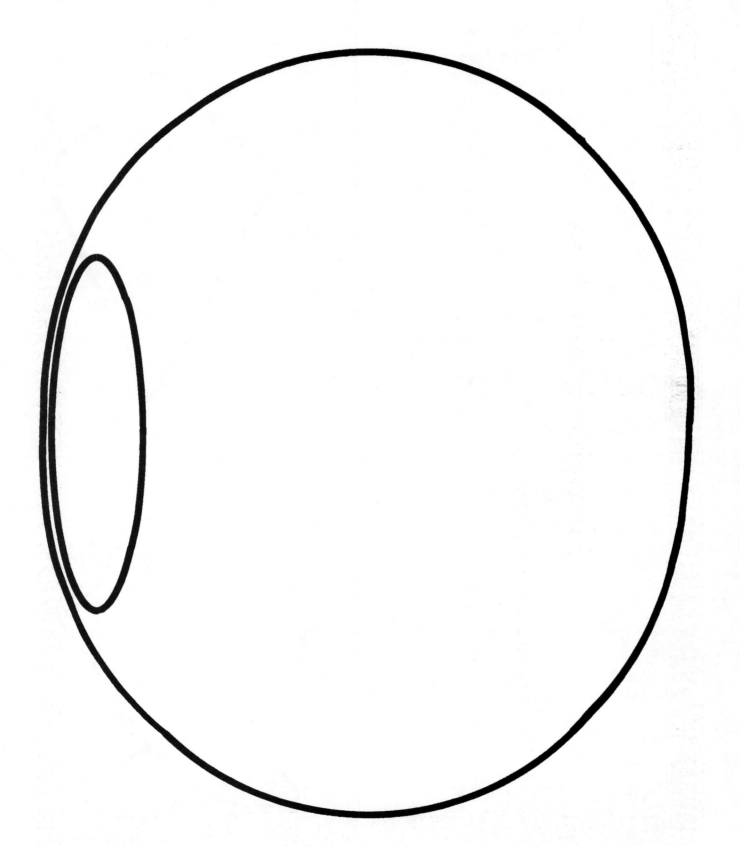

36

Favorite Memories

My favorite memories for the month of _____ include

_____

_____

_____

_____

_____

_____

_____   _____
Name   Date

Thematic Pins & Magnets

Children often seem to gravitate to animals. To make the unit more fun for youngsters, several animal patterns are provided below and on page 39. You may wish to use the larger patterns (page 39) with younger students, since these patterns are easier for little hands to work with, and the smaller patterns (below) for older students, adult helpers, and yourself.

Instructions for the puppy pin or magnet are given below. Additional directions, as well as other ideas for materials to use when creating these gifts, are provided on page 9 of the How to Use Thematic Teaching Ideas section of this book.

Supplies:

- puppy pattern (below and/or page 39)
- red vinyl
- glitter glue
- white and black liquid embroidery paint
- glue
- pin or magnetic strip, one per pattern
- other colored vinyls (optional)
- plastic eyes, two per pattern (optional)
- narrow ribbon (optional)
- yarn (optional)

Instructions:

1. Have students trace the puppy pattern onto the red vinyl.
2. Tell students to cut out the red vinyl puppy. Provide cutting assistance as needed.
3. After the vinyl puppy is cut out, allow students to use the liquid embroidery paint to draw in the details.
4. Have students use the glitter glue to create jewels in the puppy's collar.
5. Help students glue a pin or magnetic strip onto the back of the vinyl puppy.

Optional Ideas: You may wish to have students use other colored vinyls if necessary make puppies. In addition, students may wish to glue other things, such as two plastic eyes, a small ribbon for a collar, and a leash made out of yarn, onto their puppies.

September Patterns

Pets Videotaping Ideas

The general directions for how to make a Class Video Book are on page 10 of the How to Use Thematic Teaching Ideas section of this book. To begin this segment of the video, say, *This is the end of September, and our class has been studying about pets. First the children will share special pet songs and poems. Then they will introduce their stuffed pets. We hope you enjoy the first segment of our Class Video Book.*

Allow time for students to learn and practice the songs "Do Your Ears Hang Low?" and "Do Your Ears Stand High?" (below).

Videotape students reciting or singing the song for puppies called "Do Your Ears Hang Low?". Then have students recite or sing the song for cats called "Do Your Ears Stand High?". The words in both songs are very simple and full of visual imagery. Students may also wish to act out the songs.

Do Your Ears Hang Low?	**Do Your Ears Stand High?**
(Traditional)	
Do your ears hang low?	Do your ears stand high?
Do they wobble to and fro?	Can you wave them in the sky?
Can you tie them in a knot?	Can you swat them at a bee?
Can you tie them in a bow?	Can you swat them at a flea?
Can you throw them over your shoulder	Can you lay them nice and flat
Like a Continental soldier?	While you catnap on a mat?
Do your ears hang low?	Do your ears stand high?

Introduce students one at a time or allow youngsters to introduce themselves, and have them tell about a stuffed pet they have brought to school. Zoom the camera in on each student as that student shares information about the stuffed pet. Depending on the age of your students, you may wish to ask specific questions about the stuffed pets.

Possible questions include the following:

What is your pet's name?

Where did you get it?

What do you feed it?

What do you and your pet like to do together?

At the end of this videotaping segment, encourage students to look at the camera, hold up their stuffed pets, wave, and say all together, *Happy Pet Month, Mom and Dad!*

October Themes:
Five Senses and Halloween

Section Contents

Bibliography

Hopkins, T. *1001 Best Web Sites for Educators.* Teacher Created Materials, 2000.

URL updates are available at the following address:

http://www.teachercreated.com

Five Senses

Brandenberg, Aliki. *My Five Senses.* HarperCollins Children's Books, 1991.

Miller, Margaret. *My Five Senses.* Simon & Schuster's Children's, 1998.

Moncure, Jane Belk. *A Tasting Party: My Five Senses.* Child's World, 1998.

——————. *A Whiff and a Sniff: My Five Senses.* Child's World, 1997.

——————. *Clang, Boom, Bang.* Child's World, 1997.

——————. *My Eyes Are for Seeing: My Five Senses.* Child's World, 1998.

——————. *My Fingers Are for Touching: My Five Senses.* Child's World, 1997.

Let's Explore: Amazing Animals. Animal Senses. Videotape. D.K. Vision, 1996. 30 minutes.

Halloween

Bridwell, Norman. *Clifford's First Halloween.* Scholastic, 1995.

Bridwell, Norman. *Clifford's Halloween.* Scholastic, 1973.

Cannon, Janell. *Stellaluna.* Harcourt Brace, 1997.

The Magic School Bus Going Batty. Videotape. Scholastic Kid Vision, 1996. 30 minutes.

Milton, Joyce. *Bats! Creatures of the Night.* Putnam, 1993.

Sierra, Judy. *The House That Drac Built.* Harcourt Brace, 1998.

Silverman, Erica. *Big Pumpkin.* Simon & Schuster Children's, 1995.

Titherington, Jeanne. *Pumpkin Pumpkin.* William Morrow, 1990.

Activity Card #1

Activity Card #1: Mr. Tongue (Taste)

Supplies:

- small hand-held mirrors, one for every two or three students (optional)
- peppermint candies, sour lemon candies, salty pretzels; one per student
- unsweetened chocolate squares
- Mr. Tongue, one per student (page 46)
- glue
- scissors
- pencils
- crayons

WARNINGS: Ask parents if their children have any food allergies or dietary restrictions before allowing students to sample any foods. Please note that young children can choke on hard candies.

Instructions:

1. Ask students if they have ever noticed the little bumps on their tongues. Explain that these bumps are called taste buds and that they help us taste food and drinks.

2. Have students look at each other's taste buds.

3. If you have little hand-held mirrors for students to use, allow children to look at their own taste buds.

4. Teach students that the taste buds on the tip of the tongue help us taste things that are sweet, the taste buds on the sides of the tongue help us taste things that are sour, the taste buds in the middle of the tongue help us taste things that are salty, and the taste buds on the back of the tongue help us taste things that are bitter.

5. Distribute the Mr. Tongue activity sheet (page 46) to students. Review the location of the different kinds of taste buds.

6. Cut apart the unsweetened chocolate squares and break them into even smaller pieces. Allow students to sample the bitter pieces of chocolate.

7. Give each student a peppermint, a sour lemon candy, and a pretzel to eat. Allow time for youngsters to taste each of the flavors.

8. After they sample the different foods, ask children to color and cut out the food pictures at the bottom of the activity page.

9. Tell students to glue the food pictures on Mr. Tongue, according to which taste buds help us know whether the food is sweet, sour, salty, or bitter. Note that there are two lemon pictures because they go on each side of the tongue.

Extension: Invite students to draw pictures of their favorite foods. You may wish to discuss whether their favorite foods taste sweet, sour, salty, or bitter.

Activity Cards #2 and #3

Activity Card #2: My Hand (Touch)

Supplies:

- Touching Hands, one per student (page 47)
- cotton balls, one per student
- one-inch (2.5 cm) squares of aluminum foil, one per student
- one-inch (2.5 cm) squares of sandpaper, one per student
- pencils or crayons
- glue
- scissors

Instructions:

1. Have students look at their fingertips. Explain that our fingertips have small nerve endings that are very sensitive. Point out that these nerve endings help us identify how things feel when we touch them.
2. Distribute the cotton balls, aluminum foil squares, and sandpaper squares. Ask students to feel the cotton balls, foil, and sandpaper with their fingers. Describe the cotton balls as soft, the foil as smooth, and the sandpaper as rough.
3. Distribute the Touching Hands activity sheet to students. Point out the pictures of the snowman and campfire at the bottom of the page. Tell students that our fingertips can also help us know if something is cold like the snowman or hot like the campfire.
4. Have students place one hand flat on the activity sheet and trace around it.
5. Ask students to cut out the campfire and snowman pictures.
6. Have students glue the cotton ball, foil and sandpaper squares, snowman and campfire pictures onto the fingertips of the traced hands. Point out that only one object or picture goes on each fingertip.

Activity Card #3: Guessing Jars (Smell)

Supplies:

- 5–10 small glass or plastic jars with holes in the lids
- masking tape
- colored paper strips (optional)
- writing paper, one per group
- pencil
- suggested scents: crushed flower petals, orange slices, cinnamon, pine needles, sardines, vanilla extract, coffee beans, chocolate powder, soap, fish food

Instructions:

1. Before students arrive at the center, cover the outside of the jars with masking tape. As an alternative, you can tape colored paper strips around the outside of the jar. Be sure students do not see the items that you put inside the jars.
2. Allow students, one at a time, to guess what is in each jar, using only their sense of smell. Write students' guesses on a sheet of paper.
3. After all the students at the center have had a turn to guess the different scents, discuss the accuracy of their guesses.
4. Have students vote to tell which scent in the jars was their favorite. Then ask them to tell one of their favorite scents that was not in the jars.

Activity Cards #4 and #5

Activity Card #4: Listening Walk (Hearing)

Supplies:

- drawing paper, one per student
- pencils
- markers or crayons
- comfortable walking shoes

Instructions:

1. Tell students they will be going on a Listening Walk during which they will use their sense of hearing to identify noises they hear outside. Discuss outside safety rules. In addition to these rules, tell students that they are not allowed to talk while on the Listening Walk, so that everyone can concentrate on listening.

2. After walking with students around the school grounds for 10 minutes, take the children back into the classroom. Distribute the drawing paper to students.

3. Have students write their names and the date at the top of the drawing paper. On the chalkboard, write the following sentence starter: *On my Listening Walk I heard _____ .*

4. Ask students to copy the sentence from the chalkboard on the top part of the drawing paper, filling in the blank with a list of things they heard while on the Listening Walk. For younger students, you may wish to have children dictate their lists for you to write.

5. Have students draw pictures on the bottom part of the drawing paper to show some of the things they heard while on the Listening Walk.

Extension: You may wish to bind the Listening Walk pages into a class book. If so, have students draw small self-portraits to go on the front cover of the Listening Walk Class Book.

Activity Card #5: Cyclops' Eye Graph (Sight)

Supplies:

- Eye Diagram and Cyclops' Eye Graph, one per student (page 48)
- red, yellow, purple, and orange crayons
- Cyclops' Eyes, one eye per student (page 49)
- scissors

Instructions:

1. Distribute the Eye Diagram and Cyclops' Eye Graph to students. Discuss the Eye Diagram with students. Have students use red, yellow, purple, and orange crayons to color the eyes next to the labels of the horizontal axis of the graph.

2. Then say, *We're going to pretend we've discovered a Cyclops. A Cyclops is a creature that has only one large eye. In this activity, each of you will decide whether the Cyclops' eye is red, yellow, purple, or orange.*

3. Give each student a Cyclops' eye. Have students color the eye red, yellow, purple, or orange. Remind students that they should use only one color for their eyes.

4. After students have colored their Cyclops' eyes, count with children the number of eyes that are colored red, yellow, purple, and orange. Teach students how to record the data in the appropriate columns of the Cyclops' Eye Bar Graph.

Extension: Distribute copies of the Five Senses Mini-Booklet (page 50). Have students fill in the blanks, draw pictures to show what they wrote about, and cut out the mini-booklet pages. Staple the mini-booklet pages together for students.

Award Certificate

Give students the Five Senses' Special Day Award Certificate after they have completed all five center activities. You may prefer to fill in individual student names ahead of time.

✂ -

Congratulations to _____

for completing the

Five Senses' Special Day Centers!

_____   _____
            Teacher   Date

✂ -

Congratulations to _____

for completing the

Five Senses' Special Day Centers!

_____   _____
            Teacher   Date

Mr. Tongue

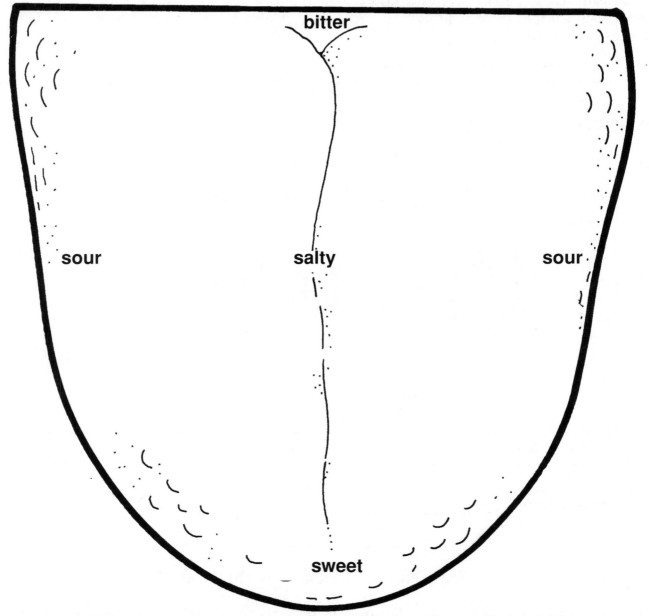

Cut out the pictures shown below, and glue them in the correct place on Mr. Tongue.

Touching Hands

Trace your hand in the space below.

Cut out the following pictures. Then glue each picture onto a fingertip of your traced hand.

campfire   snowman

Eye Diagram

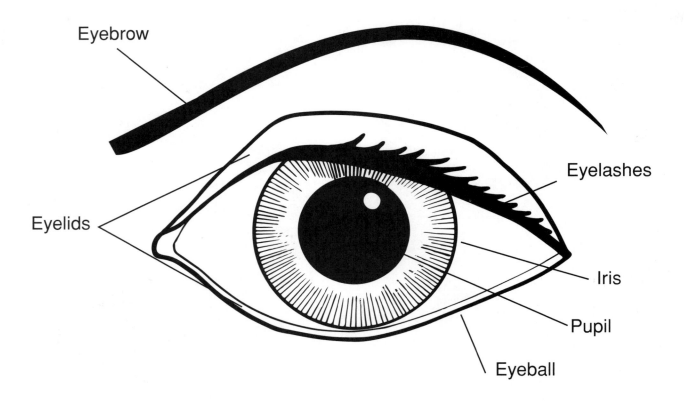

Eyebrow

Eyelashes

Eyelids

Iris

Pupil

Eyeball

Cyclops' Eye Graph

	Red	Yellow	Purple	Orange
8				
7				
6				
5				
4				
3				
2				
1				

Cyclops' Eye Colors

Cyclops' Eyes

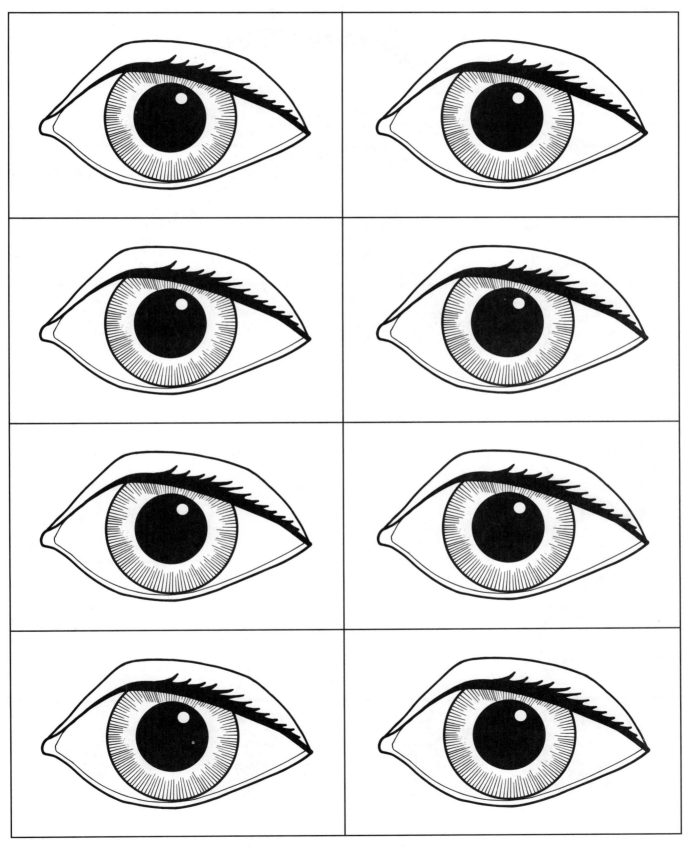

Five Senses Mini-Booklet

My Five Senses Booklet

By _____

Date: _____

My mouth likes to taste _____ .

My hands like to touch _____ .

My nose likes to smell _____ .

My ears like to hear _____ .

My eyes like to see _____ .

Snack Ideas and Recommended Book

Supplies:

- large sugar cookies, one per student
- decorative frosting in a tube, various colors
- plastic or paper cups, one per student (optional)
- paper plates
- milk (optional)
- plain index cards, one per student
- medium-sized paper bag

WARNING: Be sure to ask parents if their children have any food allergies or dietary restrictions.

Instructions:

Bake or purchase the large sugar cookies. Prepare the cookies ahead of time by using the decorative frosting to draw a simple picture of a smile and tongue, a hand, a nose, an ear, or an eye on each cookie. Place each cookie on a paper plate. Put the paper plates on a table. Be sure you have enough cookies for each child to have one. You may wish to have a few extra cookies on hand.

Examples of cookie decorations:

Ahead of time, also prepare a surprise bag by drawing a simple picture of a smile and tongue, a hand, a nose, an ear, or an eye on each index card. Be sure the drawing on each index card matches a cookie that you have prepared. For example, if you have five cookies with eyes drawn on them, then you should have five index cards with eyes drawn on them. Place the index cards in the paper bag.

After students have completed all five centers, allow each child to draw a card out of the bag. Ask students, one at a time, to identify the sense (taste, touch, smell, hearing, sight) that the picture on the index card represents and what their favorite thing is using that sense. For example, if a child picks a card with a picture of a nose, the youngster says that the sense is smell and he/she could name baking cookies as the favorite thing to smell.

Then have students, one or two at a time, go to the cookie snack table and pick a sugar cookie that has the same picture on it as the index card they took out of the bag.

You may wish to serve milk for students to drink while eating their sugar cookies.

Recommended Book: On Five Senses' Special Day, read aloud *My Five Senses* by Aliki Brandenberg (HarperCollins Children's Books, 1991).

Halloween Whole Class Activity

Supplies:

- *Big Pumpkin* written by Erica Silverman and illustrated by S.D. Schindler (Simon & Schuster Children's, 1992)
- Necklace Patterns (page 54)
- yarn or string, one piece per pattern
- hole puncher
- bat mask
- medium-sized witch's hat
- large plastic pumpkin with a handle or fake vine attached

Instructions:

1. Purchase a bat mask and witch's hat or make these out of black construction paper.

2. Read aloud the *Big Pumpkin* story to students, using dramatic expression for each of the Halloween characters.

3. Explain to students they will be acting out the story. Assign character roles and costumes to students. The witch wears a hat; the ghost, vampire, and mummy wear necklaces to match their characters; and the bat wears a bat mask.

4. Place the plastic pumpkin at the front of the classroom and have the witch character stand next to it at the beginning of the play.

5. Retell the story, and have five students at a time act it out as described below and on page 53. After the play is over, allow the five students to take a bow and get applause from the audience. Then choose five more students to perform the play. Continue presenting the play until every student in the class has had the opportunity to be in it. **Note:** It is recommended that students perform the play once per day throughout the week of Halloween.

Play

(The little witch tries to pull the pumpkin off the vine. She pulls on the handle or vine of the plastic pumpkin, but nothing happens.)

Witch: *(Jumping up and down)* Oh, drat!

Witch and Class: *(In a witch voice)* It's big and it's mine, and it's stuck on the vine, and Halloween is just hours away.

(The ghost walks up to the witch.)

Ghost: I'm bigger and stronger than you, so let me help!

(The ghost tries but cannot pull the pumpkin off the vine.)

Ghost: *(Jumping up and down)* Oh, drat!

Witch and Class: *(In a witch voice)* It's big and it's mine, and it's stuck on the vine, and Halloween is just hours away.

Play *(cont.)*

(The vampire comes up to the witch and the ghost.)

Vampire: I'm bigger and stronger than both of you, so let me help!

(The vampire tries but cannot pull the pumpkin off the vine.)

Vampire: *(Jumping up and down)* Oh, drat!

Witch and Class: *(In a witch voice)* It's big and it's mine, and it's stuck on the vine, and Halloween is just hours away.

(The mummy comes up to the witch, ghost, and vampire.)

Mummy: I'm bigger and stronger than all of you, so let me help!

(The mummy tries but cannot pull the pumpkin off the vine.)

Mummy: *(Jumping up and down)* Oh, drat!

Witch and Class: *(In a witch voice)* It's big and it's mine, and it's stuck on the vine, and Halloween is just hours away.

(The bat flies up to where the witch, ghost, vampire, and mummy are standing.)

Bat: Can I help?

(The witch, ghost, vampire, and mummy laugh.)

Bat: I might not be big and strong, but I am smart, and I have an idea!

(The witch, ghost, vampire, mummy, and bat huddle together and whisper.)

Witch, Ghost, Vampire, Mummy, and Bat: *(Excited)* Okay. Let's give it a try!

(The witch pulls on the pumpkin, the ghost pulls on the witch, the vampire pulls on the ghost, the mummy pulls on the vampire, and the bat pulls on the mummy. Suddenly the pumpkin snaps off the vine, and the witch, ghost, vampire, mummy, and bat cheer.)

(The witch rolls the pumpkin back to her house and into her kitchen, where she makes a huge pumpkin pie out of it. After the pie is cooked, the witch gives a piece of it to herself, ghost, vampire, mummy, and bat in celebration of Halloween.)

Necklace Patterns

You may wish to enlarge the patterns. Make one copy of the patterns. Cut out the ghost, vampire, and mummy. Punch a hole in the top of each. Place a piece of string or yarn through each hole to make a necklace.

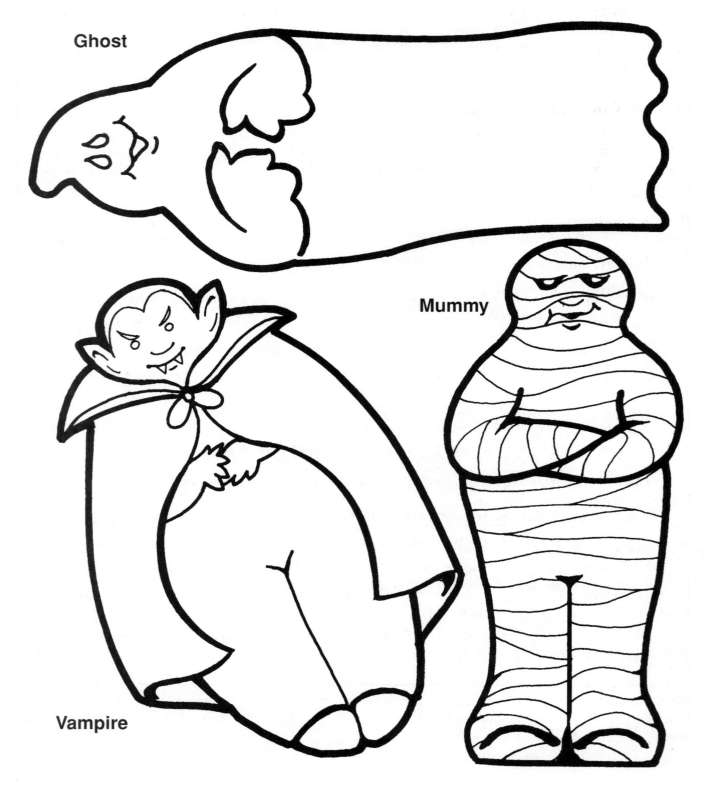

Ghost

Mummy

Vampire

Buddy Time Activities

Pinto Bean Pumpkins

Give each big and little buddy a copy of the Pinto Bean Pumpkins activity sheet (page 56) and a bowl of dry pinto beans. Have students guess how many pinto beans it will take to completely cover each pumpkin face. Tell them to record their guesses on the activity sheet. Then, one pumpkin at a time, have the buddies completely cover a pumpkin face with pinto beans, count how many beans it took to completely cover the face, and record that amount on the activity sheet. For an extension activity, have the buddies color the pumpkin faces. Then they can draw their own pumpkin faces on the back of the activity sheet.

October Concentration Game

Reproduce the Concentration Cards (page 57) on cardstock or construction paper. Make two sets of the cards for each pair of buddies. The buddies may color the pictures on the cards if they wish. Then have the buddies cut apart the cards and write their names on the back of each card. There should be four cards of each picture.

Have the buddies place their two sets of cards into a deck so they are facing the same way. Tell the buddies to mix up the cards. Have the buddies place all the cards face down on the floor or a table. Explain the following rules for playing concentration.

- The players take turns turning over two cards at a time.

- If a player turns over two cards that match, the player keeps the cards. Then that player goes again.

- If a player turns over two cards that do not match, the player must turn the cards back over. Then it is the other player's turn.

- Only two identical pictures are needed to make a match.

- The winner is the player with the most cards at the end of the game.

Extra October Card Games

Have the buddies play a fun phonics game using the Concentration Cards (page 57). Reproduce one set for each pair of buddies. Have the little buddies tell their big buddies what letter each picture name starts with.

Have the buddies play a story telling game using the Concentration Cards (page 57). Tell youngsters to place all of the cards facedown on the floor or a table. Have the buddies take turns turning over one card at a time. Ask them to use each card to tell part of a Halloween story. Remind the buddies that all of the cards together will be used to make up one story. Point out that the story ends when the last card is turned over.

When the games are over, place each set of cards in an envelope or resealable plastic bag. Write the little buddies' names on the outside of their envelopes/bags. Allow the little buddies to take their cards home.

Pinto Bean Pumpkins

Name: _____ Date: _____

First guess how many beans it will take to completely cover these pumpkin faces. Write your guesses. Then, one pumpkin at a time, completely cover a pumpkin face with pinto beans, count how many beans it took to completely cover the face, and write the number of beans you counted.

Guessed: _____

Counted: _____

Guessed: _____

Counted: _____

Guessed: _____

Counted: _____

Guessed: _____

Counted: _____

Concentration Cards

Clifford Backpack Buddy

October Theme: Halloween

Backpack Buddy: little red stuffed dog

Storybook: *Clifford's Halloween* by Norman Bridwell (Scholastic, 1973)

Supplies:
- journal
- Letter from Clifford Backpack Buddy (page 59)
- Journal Assignment, one per student (page 60)
- backpack
- Clifford Backpack Buddy

Instructions:

You may wish to make the writing journals from portfolios with fasteners. Be sure there are enough journal pages (copies of page 60) for every student in the classroom to complete the writing assignment. Inside the journal, also place a copy of the Letter from Clifford Backpack Buddy. The homework assignment is described for parents and students in this letter. However, you may prefer to explain the assignment to students before they take it home.

For this journal assignment, students read the book *Clifford's Halloween;* draw Clifford in a Halloween costume; and write a short Halloween adventure, starring Clifford.

Before sending the backpack home with a different child each day, check to be sure it has the little red stuffed dog, the book *Clifford's Halloween,* and the writing journal. Remind the student who is taking these materials home to return the backpack and its contents the next school day. When it is the next school day, allow time for the student who took the backpack home to share his/her picture of Clifford and journal writing assignment with the class.

Be sure every student has an opportunity to take the backpack home. After all students have completed the writing assignment, make the journal a permanent addition to your classroom library.

Letter from Clifford Backpack Buddy

Hi!

I'm Clifford, the red puppy from the Norman Bridwell books. I grow from a puppy into a huge red dog. In the book you are about to read, *Clifford's Halloween,* I'm trying to decide what costume to wear. Maybe you can help me out!

After you read *Clifford's Halloween,* please use a page in this journal to draw a costume for me. It can be a costume that you saw in the book, or it can be a costume that you make up. When you are done drawing my costume, write a short story about an adventure I have on Halloween night. The story has been started for you.

In the morning, please put the book *Clifford's Halloween*, this journal, and me inside the backpack and return all of these things to your teacher. You will get to share the costume you drew and your adventure story with the class, and another student will get to take me home.

Thanks for making my visit so much fun.

Happy Halloween!

Love and puppy licks,

Clifford

Journal Assignment

Name: _____ Date: _____

Here is a picture of Clifford in his Halloween Costume.

It was a spooky Halloween night. Clifford looked great in his Halloween costume as he went out the door to go trick or treating.

_____

_____

_____

_____

_____

_____

_____

_____

_____

Art & Poetry Activities

Five Senses

Supplies:

- "My Five Senses" poem and "October" title, one per student (page 62)
- Five Senses Symbols, one per student (page 63)
- large orange construction paper, one piece per student
- scissors
- glue
- old magazines
- crayons
- Favorite Memories, one per student (page 37)

Instructions:

Distribute the top half of page 62, Five Senses Symbols, and construction paper to students. Have youngsters cut out the senses symbols and glue these onto the construction paper in random order. Allow students to cut out magazine pictures that go with each of the five senses. (Examples: sunset picture — sight, telephone — hearing, rose — smell, chocolate chip cookie — taste, furry kitten — touch) Have students glue each picture next to the correct sense symbol. Point out that there may be several pictures for each symbol. Read aloud the poem "My Five Senses." Tell students to cut out the poem and "October" title. Have children glue these on top of the collage. Distribute the Favorite Memories activity sheet and help students complete it. Have students glue it onto the back of the construction paper.

Three Black Bats

Supplies:

- Halloween Night picture and bat pattern (page 64)
- black construction paper, one piece per student
- scissors
- white chalk, one piece per student
- glue
- crayons
- small plastic eyes, six per student (optional)
- large black construction paper, one piece per student
- "Three Black Bats" poem and "October" title, one per student (page 62)
- Favorite Memories, one per student (page 37)

Instructions:

Give each student a copy of Halloween Night, a piece of black construction paper, and a piece of white chalk. Have students cut out the bat pattern. Tell children to make three bats by placing the pattern on the black construction paper and tracing around it with the chalk. Have youngsters cut out the bats. Tell children to glue the bats onto the Halloween Night picture. Invite students to use crayons to add stars, pumpkins, ghosts, a full moon, etc. to the picture. You may wish to give students plastic eyes to glue onto the bats. Distribute the large black construction paper and the bottom half of page 62 to students. Read aloud the poem. Then have students cut out the poem and the "October" title. Have students glue the poem on the right half of the large black construction paper. Have them glue the Halloween picture on the left half of the construction paper. Then have them glue the "October" title so it is centered at the top of the construction paper. If students have not already done a Favorite Memories activity sheet, help them complete one now. Tell youngsters to glue the activity sheet onto the back of this artwork.

October Poems

My Five Senses

With my nose, I smell a dog.

With my eyes, I see a frog.

With my hands, I pet a cat.

With my ears, I hear a bat.

With my mouth, I taste a gnat!

Yuck! Can't you just imagine that?

Enjoy your senses, but beware

Little bugs can fly anywhere!

October

Three Black Bats

The wind blew loud on Halloween night.

Three little black bats were holding on tight.

Three little black bats hanging in a tree.

The first one yelled, "Hey, look at me!"

He spread his wings and began to fall.

All the little bats had a free for all.

They dove and swooped and had such fun

Until the rising of the sun.

Then the three little black bats went home to their tree

And hung upside down so quietly.

October

Five Senses Symbols

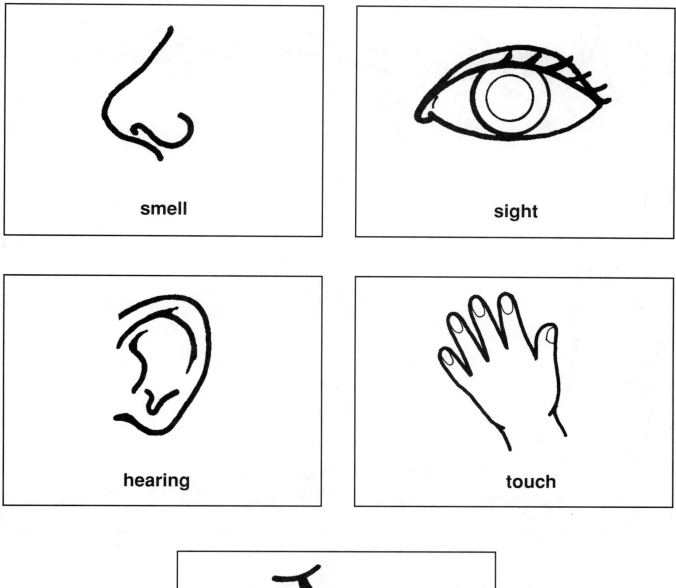

smell

sight

hearing

touch

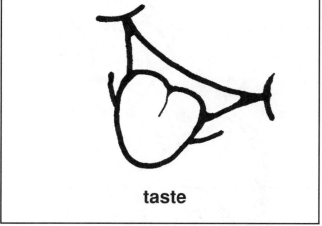

taste

Halloween Night

Name: _____ Date: _____

Thematic Pins & Magnets

Pumpkins are fun to make and are especially easy for children to design. All types of jack-o'-lantern faces can be drawn. There are several patterns provided below and on page 66. Use those that are most appropriate for your students. You may wish to use the larger patterns (below) with younger students, since these patterns are easier for little hands to work with, and the smaller patterns (page 66) for older students, adult helpers, and yourself.

Instructions for the pumpkin pin or magnet are given below. Additional directions, as well as other ideas for materials to use when creating these gifts, are provided on page 9 of the How to Use Thematic Teaching Ideas section of this book.

Supplies:

- pumpkin pattern (below and/or page 66; optional)
- orange tagboard
- black and green liquid embroidery paint
- pin or magnetic strip, one per pattern
- glue

Instructions:

1. Have students draw a pumpkin or trace one of the pumpkin patterns onto the orange tagboard.
2. Have students cut out their pumpkins.
3. Show students how to use the black embroidery paint to draw the pumpkin's facial features.
4. Allow students to use green embroidery paint to color the stem.
5. Help youngsters glue a pin or magnetic strip onto the back of the pumpkin.

October Patterns

Halloween Videotaping Ideas

The general directions for how to make a Class Video Book are on page 10 of the How to Use Thematic Teaching Ideas section of this book.

You may wish to send a note home asking parents to send their children's Halloween costumes to school or to have their children wear the costumes to school on the day of videotaping.

Ahead of time, reproduce the Pumpkin and Jack-o'-Lantern Patterns (page 68) on orange construction paper or cardstock. Have students cut out the two patterns and glue the back of the jack-o'-lantern pattern to the back of the pumpkin pattern.

Allow time for students to learn and practice "The Pumpkin Song" (below).

To begin this segment of the video, say, *This is the month of October and in our classroom we have some special visitors who are going to sing The Pumpkin Song for you. We hope you enjoy this segment of our Class Video Book.*

Then videotape students singing "The Pumpkin Song." Have students show their pumpkins and jack-o'-lanterns as indicated in the song.

The Pumpkin Song
(Traditional)
Tune: Have You Ever Seen

Once I had a pumpkin, a pumpkin, a pumpkin.
Oh, once I had a pumpkin with no face at all!
With no eyes and no nose and no mouth and no teeth.
Oh, once I had a pumpkin with no face at all!
(Students show their pumpkins.)

So I made a jack-o'-lantern, a jack-o'-lantern, a jack-o'-lantern.
So I made a jack-o'-lantern with a BIG funny face!
With BIG eyes and a BIG nose and a BIG mouth and BIG teeth.
So I made a jack-o'-lantern with a BIG funny face!
(Students show their jack-o'-lanterns.)

Introduce students one at a time or allow children to introduce themselves. If students are wearing their costumes, ask youngsters to explain what their costumes are. If students are not wearing their costumes, ask children to tell what their costumes will be. As an alternative, you may prefer to have students draw a picture of their costumes. Then zoom the camera in on each picture as individual students describe their costumes.

To complete this videotaping segment, encourage students to look at the camera, wave, and say all together, *Happy Halloween, Mom and Dad!*

Pumpkin and Jack-o'-Lantern Patterns

Cut out the two patterns. Then glue the back of the jack-o'-lantern pattern to the back of the pumpkin pattern.

November Themes:
Native Americans and Thanksgiving

Section Contents

Bibliography

Hopkins, T. *1001 Best Web Sites for Educators.* Teacher Created Materials, 2000.

URL updates are available at the following address: http://www.teachercreated.com

Native Americans

The Adventures of Pocahontas. Videotape. Good Times Home Video, Corp., 1994. 50 minutes.

Brown, Margaret Wise. *David's Little Indian.* Hyperion Books for Children, 1992.

De Paola, Tomie. *The Legend of Indian Paintbrush.* Putnam, 1991.

Emanuels, George. *California Indians.* Diablo Books, 1991.

Grossman, Virginia. *Ten Little Rabbits.* Chronicle Books, 1995.

Kessel, Joyce K. *Squanto and the First Thanksgiving.* Lerner, 1986.

Liptak, Karen. *North American Indian Sign Language.* Franklin Watts, 1993.

Martin, Rafe. *The Rough-Face Girl.* Putnam, 1998.

Thanksgiving

Bridwell, Norman. *Clifford's Thanksgiving Visit.* Scholastic, 1993.

Bunting, Eve. *A Turkey for Thanksgiving.* Houghton-Mifflin, 1997.

Hallinan, P.K. *I'm Thankful Each Day!* Hambleton-Hill Publishing, 1992.

Hap Palmer's Holiday Music. Cassette or CD. Educational Activities, 1999.

Hayward, Linda. *The First Thanksgiving.* Random House, 1990.

Molly's Pilgrim. Videotape. Phoenix/BFA Films and Video, 1989. 30 minutes.

Pilkey, Dav. *'Twas the Night Before Thanksgiving.* Orchard Books, 1990.

Introduction to the Native Americans' Special Day

To help students understand the incredible diversity among the Native American tribes in North America, read aloud these two wonderful primary books: *The Very First Americans* by Cara Ashrose (Putnam Publishing Group, 1993) and *Native Americans* by Jay Miller (Grolier Publishing, 1993). You may wish to share these with students before the Special Day center activities begin. These books have beautiful illustrations and help to explain the various lifestyles and customs of the major North American indigenous peoples.

The Special Day activities included in this section are suggested as a closure event for the month of November. To give students additional information about Native Americans, place one of the nonfiction primary books suggested below at each center. These books could be read before or after the activities at the centers. If time is limited, the nonfiction books could be shared while students are working on their center projects.

Suggested nonfiction primary Native American books:

Ashrose, Cara. *The Very First Americans.* Putnam, 1993.

McKissach, Patricia. *The Apache: A New True Book.* Children's Press, 1984. (Out of print)

Miller, Jay. *American Indian Families: A New True Book.* Children's Press, 1997.

Miller, Jay. *American Indian Foods: A New True Book.* Children's Press, 1997.

Miller, Jay. *Native Americans: A New True Book.* Grolier, 1993.

Roop, Peter Geiger and Connie. *If You Lived with the Cherokee.* Scholastic, 1998.

Sneve, Virginia Driving Hawk. *The Sioux.* Holiday House, 1993.

Activity Cards #1 and #2

Activity Card #1: Native American Drums

Supplies:

- empty coffee cans or hot chocolate cans with plastic lids, one per student
- yarn or string, one piece per student
- scissors
- markers
- white contact paper or white construction paper
- glue (optional)
- colored plastic tape
- "The Beating Drum Song," one per student (page 75)

Instructions:

1. Ahead of time, cover the cans with white contact paper or by gluing white construction paper around them. If construction paper is used, allow time for the glue to dry.
2. Give each student a can. Tell children that they are going to make Native American drums out of the cans.
3. Have students use the markers to draw designs on their drums.
4. Be sure students write their names on their drums.
5. Help students attach yarn or string to their drums by encircling the can with the colored plastic tape.

Extension: Invite students to play their drums while singing "The Beating Drum Song."

Activity Card #2: Native American Poem and Puppet

Supplies:

- Native American Poem and Puppet, one per student (page 76)
- small paper bags, one per student
- crayons or markers
- scissors
- glue
- real feathers (optional)
- Native American Names, one per student (page 77)

Instructions:

1. Give each student a copy of the Native American Poem and Puppet activity sheet and a paper bag.
2. Have students color and cut out the puppet.
3. Tell students to turn the paper bag upside down without opening it. Show them how to glue the puppet's head onto the bottom of the bag. Then show them how to glue the puppet's body on the side of the bag. If real feathers are available, have students glue these to the puppet's headband.
4. Read aloud the poem to students. Have students glue the poem on the back of the paper bag.
5. Teach students how to open and close the puppet's mouth as they recite the poem.
6. Ask students to give Native American names to their puppets by choosing from the list on page 77 or by making them up.

Activity Cards #3 and #4

Activity Card #3: Pinch Pots and Buffalo Hide Drawings

Supplies:

- wet ceramic potter's clay, preferably brick or red colored
- resealable plastic bags, one per student
- small paper plates, one per student
- pencils
- large brown paper grocery bags
- Buffalo Hide Pattern (page 78)
- scissors
- markers or small bottles of fabric paint, several different colors
- Native American Symbols, one per student (pages 79 and 80)

Instructions:

1. Ahead of time form the clay into balls (about the size of tennis balls), one per student. Place the balls of clay in resealable plastic bags to keep them moist.
2. Also ahead of time, trace the Buffalo Hide Pattern onto the paper bags. (Several patterns will fit on each bag.) Cut out the "buffalo hides" from the paper bags.
3. Give the clay to students. Have children make clay pinch pots by pressing their thumbs down in the middle of the clay ball to make the bowl indentations. Have students use a pencil to etch their names in the bottoms of their pots.
4. Have students place their pinch pots on small paper plates. Allow the clay to dry.
5. Distribute the paper bag buffalo hides and Native American Symbols to students. Have youngsters decorate their buffalo hides using markers or fabric paints. Encourage students to paint or draw real Native American symbols.

Extension: Invite students to look at books about Native American customs.

Activity Card #4: Native American Trail Mix

Supplies:

- chocolate or carob chips
- raisins
- peanuts or dried fruit
- fish-shaped crackers
- large bowl
- small paper cups, one per student
- Trail Mix Graph, one per student (page 81)

WARNING: Ask parents if their children have any food allergies or dietary restrictions.

Instructions:

1. In a large bowl, mix together the chocolate or carob chips, raisins, peanuts or dried fruit, and fish-shaped crackers. Scoop some trail mix into each cup.
2. Give each student a cup of trail mix. Tell students not to eat the trail mix until they are done with the activity.
3. Distribute the Trail Mix Graph to students. Ask students to sort and count the ingredients in the trail mix. Show students how to record this information on the bar graph. Students may need to count by twos or fives on their graph. Show them how to mark the vertical scale accordingly.
4. After students have completed the graph, allow them to eat their trail mix.

Extension: Invite students to make up their own trail mix recipes.

Activity Card #5

Activity Card #5: Headbands and Necklaces

Supplies:

- 20" x 4" (50 cm x 10.5 cm) tagboard strips, one per student
- brightly colored markers
- real feathers, two or three per child
- cellophane tape
- stapler and staples
- large dyed macaroni or plastic or wooden beads (**Note:** Beads may be purchased from a craft store.)
- necklace-length brown yarn long enough to fit over head, one piece per student
- scissors
- stapler and staples

Instructions:

1. Ahead of time, fold the tagboard strips in half the long way. In addition, prepare the yarn by cutting it to necklace-length pieces, one per student. Tie a knot around a piece of macaroni or a bead at one end of the yarn. This will make it easier for students to string the rest of the macaroni or beads.

2. Give each student a tagboard strip. Tell students to place the strip in front of them with the open part at the top and the fold at the bottom.

   Example:

3. Explain to students that they will use the tagboard strips to make Native American headbands. Tell students to use the markers to make colorful patterns on their tagboard headbands.

4. Have students choose two or three real feathers. Help youngsters tape one end of each feather inside the fold of the headband.

5. To make the headband, wrap the tagboard strip so it fits comfortably around a child's head. Carefully remove the headband from the child's head without changing the size. Staple the ends in place. Then give it back to the youngster.

6. Give each student a piece of yarn with the macaroni or bead already tied onto it.

7. Have students make their necklaces by stringing additional pieces of macaroni or beads. They may wish to make a pattern with their macaroni or beads.

8. When students are done stringing the macaroni or beads, help youngsters tie the ends of the yarn together.

9. Invite students to wear their headbands and necklaces.

Extension: Students might enjoy making extra necklaces or bracelets.

Award Certificate

Give students the Native Americans' Special Day Award Certificate after they have completed all five center activities. You may prefer to fill in individual student names ahead of time.

✂ -

Congratulations to _____

for completing the

Native Americans' Special Day Centers!

_____   _____
Teacher   Date

✂ -

Congratulations to _____

for completing the

Native Americans' Special Day Centers!

_____   _____
Teacher   Date

74

The Beating Drum Song

(Traditional Chant)

This is how a big strong Indian

beats upon his drum ...

Ho Ho Hi Hi Ho Ho Hi.

This is how a big strong Indian

hunts a buffalo ...

Ho Ho Hi Hi Ho Ho Hi.

This is how a big strong Indian

builds his own teepee ...

Ho Ho Hi Hi Ho Ho Hi.

This is how a big strong Indian

paddles his canoe ...

Ho Ho Hi Hi Ho Ho Hi.

This is how a big strong Indian

beats upon his drum ...

Ho Ho Hi Hi Ho Ho Hi.

Native American Poem and Puppet

Native American Poem

I'm a little Indian with feathers in my hair.

Here's my bow and arrow that flies through the air.

I sleep inside a teepee and fish in a lake for trout.

And when I'm very happy, I dance and sing and shout!

WOOOOOOOOOO!

Native American Puppet

Native American Names

Black Raven	Bright Sun	Running Brook
Brave Fox	Eagle Feather	Running Deer
Brave Heart	Little Bear	Running Path
Brave Hunter	Little Beaver	Running Water
Brave One	Little Buffalo	Straight Arrow
Bright Lightning	Pure Heart	Strong Buffalo
Bright Moon	Red Hawk	Wise Owl

Buffalo Hide Pattern

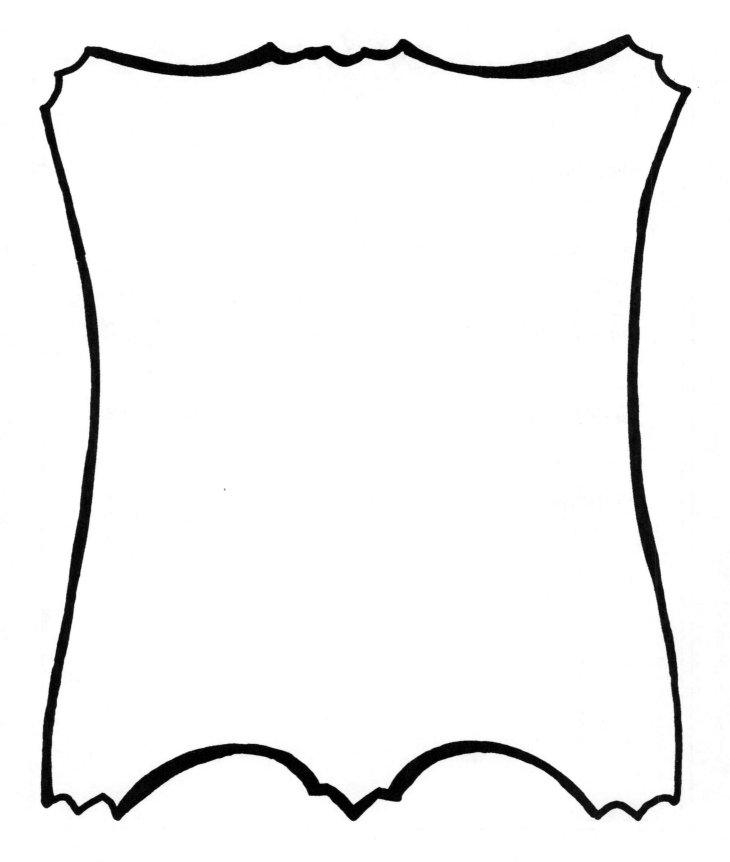

Native American Symbols

war

feast

Indian chief

rain

lake

bird tracks

day

peace pipe

to hunt

summer

deer

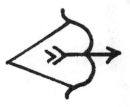

horse tracks

Native American Symbols

campfire

lightning

mountain pass

corn

leaving teepee

night

III-⊕

3 days

rainbow

forest

river

war bonnet

day

Trail Mix Graph

Name: _____ Date: _____

	Chocolate or Carob Chips	Raisins	Peanuts/ Dried Fruit	Fish-Shaped Crackers

Snack Ideas and Recommended Book

Supplies:

- Native American Drums (Activity Card #1, page 71)
- "The Beating Drum Song," one per student (page 75)
- Native American Poem and Puppet (Activity Card #2, page 71; page 76)
- popcorn
- air popcorn popper (optional)
- large bowl (optional)
- salt (optional)
- small paper bags or large paper cups, one per student
- small plastic or paper cups, one per student
- juice

WARNINGS: Be sure to ask parents if their children have any food allergies or dietary restrictions before serving a snack. Do not allow students near the hot popcorn popper.

Instructions:

For Native Americans' Special Day, after students have completed the five centers, have them perform "The Beating Drum Song." Then have them recite the Native American Poem, using their puppets.

Pop the popcorn into a large bowl. Salt the popcorn if desired. If you prefer, the popcorn can be popped ahead of time, or you can purchase prepopped popcorn.

For each student, fill a small paper bag or large paper cup with popcorn. Give the popcorn to students. Tell the class that Native Americans were the first to pop corn in their fire pits, and these people taught the early pioneers how to do this.

If you are serving juice, pour some into the small cups for students.

Recommended Book: On Native Americans' Special Day, read aloud *The Rough-Face Girl* written by Rafe Martin and illustrated by David Shannon (Putnam Publishing Group, 1998). It is a beautiful Native American legend, similar to the Cinderella story.

Thanksgiving Whole Class Activity

Supplies:

- *'Twas the Night Before Thanksgiving* by Dav Pilkey (Orchard Books, 1990)
- 1' x 1' (30 cm x 30 cm) pieces of white cotton fabric, one square per student
- 1' x 1' (30 cm x 30 cm) pieces of colorful fabric
- fabric crayons, several boxes
- quilt batting (**Note:** The size will vary depending on the number of students making quilt squares.)
- plain fabric, different solid colors (**Note:** The size will vary depending on the number of students making quilt squares.)
- iron
- sewing machine

Instructions:

Read aloud the story *'Twas the Night Before Thanksgiving* by Dav Pilkey. This book is a wonderful poem about children going on a field trip to a turkey farm. The format of this story is similar to *'Twas the Night Before Christmas*. Students might enjoy comparing and contrasting these two holiday stories.

After reading *'Twas the Night Before Thanksgiving,* discuss the plot with students, emphasizing how thankful the turkeys must have been when the children in the story saved them. Next have students brainstorm a list of things for which they are thankful. Record students' ideas on a white board, chalkboard, or large blank piece of paper. Display the list in the classroom so students can refer back to it when they are doing the following activity.

Give each student a square of white fabric. Tell students that they must leave a one-inch (2.5 cm) border all the way around the fabric square so that the pieces can be sewn together to make a quilt. Have students use the fabric crayons to draw three or more things for which they are thankful. Tell students to write their names near the bottom of the squares. Make sure they do not write in the border.

You may wish to enlist the help of one or more parent volunteers to iron the squares (according to directions on the fabric crayon boxes), to sew the squares together, and to sew the squares to the plain fabric backing (with the quilt batting in between). When sewing the front of the quilt together, alternate students' decorated fabric squares with the colorful squares. On one white fabric square, write the title, "We Are Thankful for. . . ." When sewing the front of the quilt together, place the title at the top, in the middle.

The Thanksgiving quilt makes a beautiful wall hanging that can be displayed in the classroom or school library. At the end of the year, you may wish to donate the quilt to a charity or auction it off at a school carnival or fundraiser. As an alternative, the quilt also makes a nice gift for a special parent or classroom volunteer. For example, it could be given to an adopted grandmother or grandfather who visits your classroom and reads to or works with students on a regular basis. This quilt represents the true meaning of Thanksgiving and is a wonderful culminating activity for the Thanksgiving Unit.

Buddy Time Activities

Native American Symbol Cards

Use large plain index cards and the Native American Symbols (pages 79 and 80) to create a class set of Native American Symbol Cards. Write the meaning of a symbol at the bottom of a card in small letters. Then draw that symbol, making it as large as possible. Continue in this manner until you have one card for each pair of buddies.

Give each pair of buddies a Native American Symbol Card, a bowl of dry pinto beans, and a bottle of white glue. Tell the buddies to write their names on the index cards. Have the buddies work together to cover the lines of the symbol with glue and pinto beans that are placed close together. Tell youngsters that a thick line of glue works best to hold the weight of the pinto beans. As an alternative, you may wish to allow students to use a variety of dry beans. After the beans have been placed on the symbols, store the cards on a flat surface, and allow the glue to dry overnight. Be sure that the cards do not overlap each other while the glue is drying. After the glue has dried, display the Native American Symbol Cards in the classroom. The display can be used as a decoration and as a learning tool. Have the buddies point to their cards and tell what their symbols represent.

Extension: Have the buddies write stories using the symbols on the Native American Symbol Cards.

Thankful Turkeys

Distribute markers, colored construction paper, scissors, glue, and copies of Thankful Turkeys (page 85) to the buddies. Ask the little buddies to name things they are thankful for, while the big buddies use markers to record these responses on the tail feathers of the turkey. Have big and little buddies work together to color and cut out the turkey. Then have the buddies glue the turkey to a piece of construction paper. You may wish to display the turkeys or save them for a class book.

Turkey Handprints

Provide each pair of buddies with two copies of My Turkey Handprint (page 86). Have the big buddies trace around one of their hands on a copy of My Turkey Handprint. Then have the big buddies trace around one of their little buddies' hands on the other copy of My Turkey Handprint. Tell the buddies to color their own traced hands, turning the finger outlines into turkey feathers and the thumb outline into a turkey head. Tell students that dialogue is when two or more people are carrying on a conversation. Point out that in cartoons, dialogue is often written in a bubble. You may wish to draw a cartoon bubble on the chalkboard or invite a big buddy to draw one for the class. Tell the buddies that each of them should draw a cartoon bubble next to the turkey's beak. Ask the buddies to write dialogue in these bubbles to show what the two turkeys are saying to each other.

Thankful Turkeys

Color and cut out the turkey. Then glue the turkey onto a piece of construction paper.

I am thankful for…

My Turkey Handprint

Name: _____ Date: _____

Turkey Backpack Buddy

November Theme: Thanksgiving

Backpack Buddy: small stuffed toy turkey

Storybook: *A Turkey for Thanksgiving* by Eve Bunting (Houghton-Mifflin, 1997)

Supplies:
- journal
- Letter from Turkey Backpack Buddy (page 88)
- Journal Assignment, one per student (page 89)
- backpack
- Turkey Backpack Buddy

Instructions:

You may wish to make the writing journals from portfolios with fasteners. Be sure there are enough journal pages (copies of page 89) for every student in the classroom to complete the writing assignment. Also place a copy of the Letter from Turkey Backpack Buddy inside the journal. The homework assignment is described for parents and students in this letter. However, you may prefer to explain the assignment to students before they take it home.

For this journal assignment, students read the book *A Turkey for Thanksgiving*. Then they list and draw some things for which they are thankful.

Before sending the backpack home with a different child each day, check to be sure it has the small stuffed toy turkey, the book *A Turkey for Thanksgiving,* and the writing journal. Remind the student who is taking these materials home to return the backpack and its contents the next school day. When it is the next school day, allow time for the student who took the backpack home to share his/her journal writing assignment with the class.

Be sure every student has an opportunity to take the backpack home. After all students have completed the writing assignment, make the journal a permanent addition to your classroom library.

Letter from Turkey Backpack Buddy

Gobble-gobble, gobble-gobble!

Hello! I'm the kind and polite Backpack Buddy who wanted to spend the night with you and your family during this Thanksgiving season. I'm a pet turkey who loves children. Enclosed is one of my favorite Thanksgiving stories. It is called *A Turkey for Thanksgiving.* After you and your parents read the book, you might be able to tell why a turkey like me enjoys this story so much.

This time of year is called fall, and I love it. I also love to think about all the things I am thankful for. What about you? Can you think of some things you are thankful for this year? After you read *A Turkey for Thanksgiving,* use a page in this journal to write down some of the things you are thankful for, and then draw some pictures to go with your list.

Speaking of being thankful, thanks so much for letting me spend the night at your house. I am having a great time!

Gobble-gobble,

Little Turkey

P.S. Please remember to return the book *A Turkey for Thanksgiving,* the writing journal, my backpack, and me so someone else in your class can take me home.

Journal Assignment

Name: _____ Date: _____

Here are some things for which I am thankful:

_____

_____

_____

_____

_____

_____

_____

_____

Here are some pictures of things for which I am thankful.

Art & Poetry Activities

Rolling Thunder

Supplies:

- parched paper or tan construction paper, one piece per student and one for demonstration
- Buffalo Hide Pattern (page 78, optional)
- "Rolling Thunder" poem and "November" title, one per student (top half of page 91)
- watercolor paints, one set per student
- plastic or Styrofoam bowls, one for every two students
- water
- watercolor paintbrushes
- black markers, one per student
- large orange or yellow construction paper, one piece per student
- scissors
- glue
- Favorite Memories, one per student (page 37)

Instructions:

Ahead of time, cut the parched or tan paper into buffalo hide shapes. You may wish to use the pattern provided on page 78. Distribute the materials listed above. Read the poem "Rolling Thunder" to the class. Show students how to use the watercolors to paint a rainbow on a "buffalo hide." Then have students paint a rainbow on their paper buffalo hides. Next ask students to use the black markers to draw things described in the poem "Rolling Thunder." Have students cut out the poem and the "November" title. Have them glue the buffalo hide on one half of the orange or yellow construction paper. Then have them glue the "November" title so it is centered at the top of the orange construction paper. Tell students to glue the poem on the other half. Help students complete the Favorite Memories activity sheet. Then have students glue it onto the back of the construction paper.

My Turkey Hands

Supplies:

- white construction paper, one piece per student
- real bird feathers, eight per student
- plastic eyes, one per student (optional)
- glue
- markers
- scissors
- "My Turkey Hands" poem and "November" title, one per student (bottom half of page 91)
- large orange or yellow construction paper, one piece per student
- Favorite Memories, one per student (page 37)

Instructions:

Distribute the materials listed above. Help youngsters trace both of their hands (one at a time) on the white construction paper. Ask students to glue real feathers inside the outline of the fingers. Have children use markers to draw the turkey's face on the thumb outline. If plastic eyes are available, allow students to glue an eye onto the turkey's face. Read aloud the poem "My Turkey Hands." Then have students cut out the poem and the "November" title. Have them glue the picture on the other half of the construction paper. Then have them glue the "November" title so it is centered at the top of the construction paper. Have students glue the poem on the other half of the construction paper. If students have not already done a Favorite Memories activity sheet, help them complete one now. Tell youngsters to glue the activity sheet onto the back of this artwork.

November Poems

Rolling Thunder

Rolling thunder, falling rain

Beats upon the buffalo plain.

My teepee keeps me warm and dry.

An eagle vision lights up the sky.

Then a rainbow silently appears

Reminding me the Great Spirit is here.

So on buffalo skin stretched tight

I paint these visions of the night.

November

My Turkey Hands

My hands have legs and feathers, too;

They have a beak and can gobble at you!

These turkeys are going to fly away

And not get caught on Thanksgiving Day!

November

Thematic Pins & Magnets

For the month of November, the Thanksgiving season is represented by a turkey pin or magnet. Other November patterns have also been included for students of all ages to enjoy. You may wish to use the larger patterns (page 93) with younger students, since these patterns are easier for little hands to work with, and the smaller patterns (below) for older students, adult helpers, and yourself.

Instructions for the turkey pin or magnet are given below. Additional directions, as well as other ideas for materials to use when creating these gifts, are provided on page 9 of the How to Use Thematic Teaching Ideas section of this book.

Supplies:

- turkey pattern (below and/or page 93)
- brown vinyl
- blue, green, and red liquid fabric paint
- glitter glue
- black permanent markers, one per student
- plastic eyes, two per pattern
- pin or magnetic strip, one per pattern
- glue

Instructions:

1. Have students trace the turkey pattern onto the brown vinyl.
2. Tell students to cut out the vinyl turkeys.
3. Ask students to use the black markers to draw details on the vinyl turkey.
4. Have students use the following sequence to color the turkey feathers: paint the first feather with blue liquid fabric paint, the second feather with green liquid fabric paint and the third feather with glitter glue. Tell students to follow this pattern until all of the feathers have been colored.
5. Have children use the red liquid fabric paint to make the turkey's wattle.
6. Allow the paint and glue to dry.
7. Help students glue on the turkey's plastic eyes.
8. Then help children glue a pin or magnetic strip onto the back of the vinyl turkeys.

November Patterns

Thanksgiving Videotaping Ideas

The general directions for how to make a Class Video Book are on page 10 of the How to Use Thematic Teaching Ideas section of this book.

Ahead of time, have some students make Native American headbands (page 95) and other students make Pilgrim hats (page 96). Reproduce the patterns on cardstock or white construction paper. Have students use crayons or markers to color the hats and headbands. Cut 20" x 2" (50 cm x 5 cm) tagboard strips, one per student. To make each headband, wrap a tagboard strip so it fits comfortably around a child's head. Carefully remove the headband from the child's head without changing the size. Staple the ends in place. Then staple the youngster's Native American headband or Pilgrim hat onto the tagboard headband. Give the completed headband to the student.

In addition, obtain a copy of *Hap Palmer's Holiday Music* cassette or CD (Educational Activities, 1999). Teach students the song "I Am Thankful" from this recording. Preselect certain students for the solo parts. Allow plenty of time for the class to practice singing the song before you start videotaping.

Introduce the Thanksgiving Unit video segment using a stuffed toy turkey or a turkey puppet. Have the turkey welcome the viewers by saying, *Hello! Welcome to the month of November. I'm the little class pet for this month. Today, students have changed themselves into Pilgrims and Native Americans, and they will sing "I Am Thankful," which is a song from* Hap Palmer's Holiday Music.

Videotape students singing "I Am Thankful" while they wear the Pilgrim hats and Native American headbands. Next have students introduce themselves and tell something for which they are thankful. You may wish to have students hold up the I Am Thankful activity sheet (page 89) to show pictures of things for which they are thankful.

At the end of this videotaping session, have the children look at the camera and say all together *Happy Thanksgiving, Mom and Dad!* Then zoom the camera in on students as they wave good-bye.

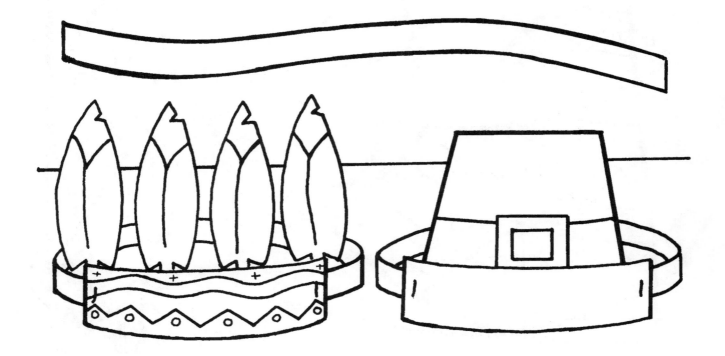

Native American Headband Pattern

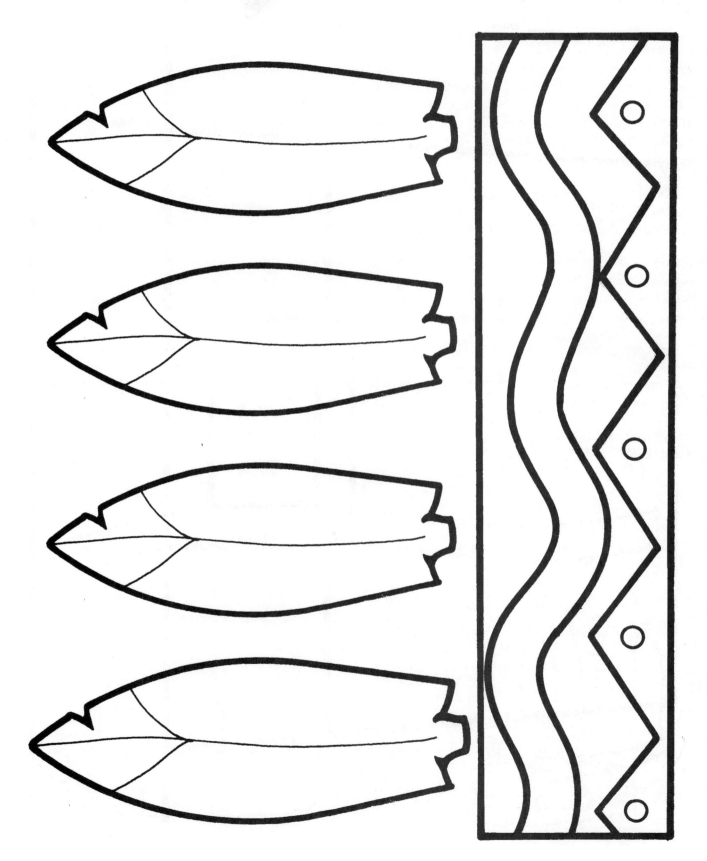

Pilgrim Hat Pattern

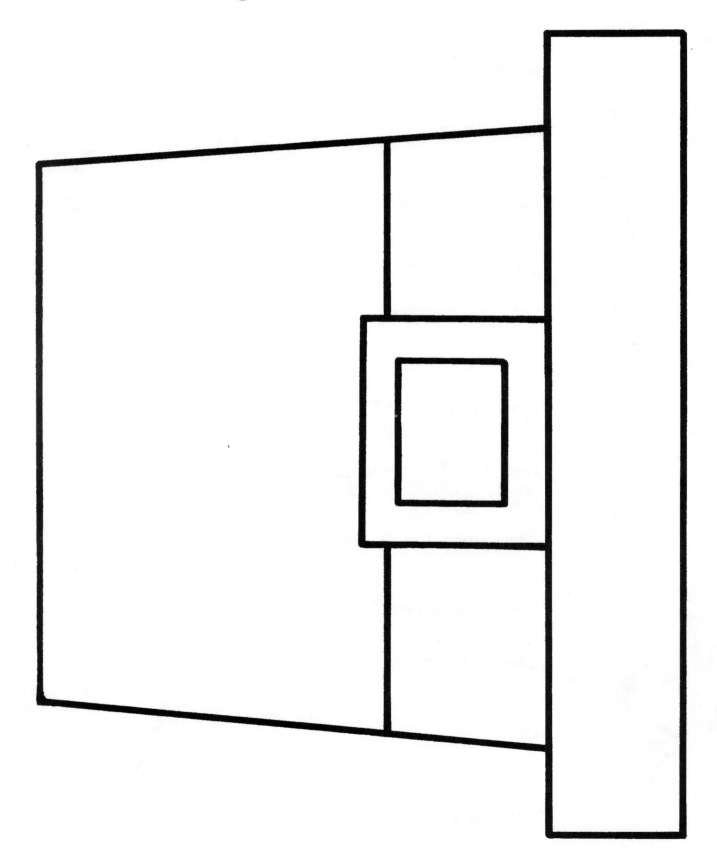

December Themes:
Frosty the Snowman and Christmas

Section Contents

Bibliography

Hopkins, T. *1001 Best Web Sites for Educators.* Teacher Created Materials, 2000. URL updates are available at the following address:

http://www.teachercreated

Frosty the Snowman

Bielitz, Joan. *Frosty the Snowman's Best Snowy Day Book.* Pocket Books, 1985. (Out of print)

Books, Emma K. *Frosty the Snowman (A Musical Board Book).* HarperCollins, 1994.

Bridwell, Norman. *Clifford's First Snow Day.* Scholastic, 1998.

Briggs, Raymond. *The Snowman (Early Step into Reading).* Random House, 1999.

Cuyler, Margery. *The Biggest, Best Snowman.* Scholastic, 1998.

The Snowman. Videotape. Columbia Tristar Home Video, 1993. 30 minutes.

Christmas

Bridwell, Norman. *Clifford's Christmas.* Scholastic, 1985.

Buss, Nancy. *The Littlest Christmas Elf.* Golden Books, 1995.

Jordan, Sandra. *Christmas Tree Farm.* Orchard Books, 1996.

Lankford, Mary D. *Christmas Around the World.* William Morrow, 1998.

May, Robert L. *Rudolph the Red-Nosed Reindeer.* Western, 1993.

Radzinski, Kandy. *The Twelve Cats of Christmas.* Scholastic, 1996.

Rudolph the Red-Nosed Reindeer. Videotape. Family Home Entertainment, 1964. 55 minutes.

Zolotow, Charlotte. *The Beautiful Christmas Tree.* Horn Book, 1999.

Activity Cards #1 and #2

Activity Card #1: Snowman Paperweights

Supplies:

- rocks that are flat or semiflat and about 3–4" (8–10 cm) in diameter, one per student
- white spray paint or water-based paint
- paintbrushes (optional)
- Snowman Rock Drawing (page 102)
- medium-point black permanent markers, one per student
- felt (optional)
- glue (optional)

Instructions:

1. Ahead of time, cover the tops of the rocks with white spray paint. As an alternative, you can use paintbrushes to apply white water-based paint. Allow the paint to dry.
2. For very young students, display the Snowman Rock Drawing.
3. Give each student a rock and black permanent marker.
4. Have students use the markers to draw a snowman on their rocks. Tell students who are very young that they can refer to the Snowman Rock Drawing.
5. You may wish to glue a piece of felt to the bottom of each rock.
6. Ask students to write their names on the bottom or side of their rocks.
7. Encourage youngsters to take home the snowman paperweights.

Activity Card #2: Pin the Carrot Nose on Frosty

Supplies:

- Bulletin Board Snowman Pattern (page 103)
- 3–4' (0.9–1.2 m) piece of butcher paper
- laminator and laminating film
- stapler and staples
- Carrot Nose Patterns, one pattern per student (page 104)
- orange paper
- scissors
- cellophane tape
- large handkerchief or scarf
- snowman stickers (optional)
- carrot sticks (optional)

WARNING: Ask parents if their children have any food allergies or dietary restrictions before serving carrot sticks as a snack.

Instructions:

1. Ahead of time, enlarge the Bulletin Board Snowman on butcher paper so it is 3–4 feet (0.9–1.2 m) tall. Then laminate the butcher paper snowman and staple it onto a bulletin board. Be sure it is low enough for students to reach Frosty's face.
2. Reproduce the Carrot Nose Patterns on orange paper and cut out the carrots.
3. When students arrive at the center, explain how to play Pin the Nose on Frosty.
4. Tie a handkerchief or scarf to blindfold a student. Give that student a carrot nose with a piece of tape stuck at the top. Have that child try to tape the carrot nose in the correct place on Frosty's face.
5. Have students take turns being blindfolded and taping a nose on Frosty's face.
6. You may wish to serve carrot sticks for a snack and give each student a snowman sticker for participating.

Activity Card #3

Activity Card #3: Snowball Toss

Supplies:

- 5–10 beanbags or balls made from aluminum foil wrapped in masking tape
- masking tape
- three large index cards
- three lined waste paper baskets
- Snowball Toss Scorecards, one card per student (page 105)
- scissors

WARNINGS: Allow plenty of space for this activity. Tell students that they should not cross the playing area. Have only one student participate at a time.

Instructions:

1. If you do not have any beanbags, you can easily make balls by wadding up pieces of aluminum foil and wrapping them in masking tape.
2. Write the following labels on index cards: *1 Point, 2 Points,* and *3 Points.*
3. Use a piece of masking tape to mark a place on the floor from which students will throw the beanbags or aluminum balls.
4. Use masking tape to attach one index card label to each waste paper basket. Stagger placement of the waste paper baskets so that the can labeled *1 Point* is closest to the masking tape line on the floor, the can labeled *3 Points* is farthest from the line, and the can marked *2 Points* is about halfway between the other two cans.
5. Cut apart the scorecards.
6. When students come to the center, show them the beanbags or aluminum foil balls. Ask youngsters to pretend the beanbags or foil balls are snowballs.
7. Give each student a Snowball Toss Scorecard. Have students write their names on their scorecards.
8. Point to each can and tell students how many points they get when they throw a "snowball" into that basket.
9. Have students take turns throwing 5–10 snowballs into the baskets. Be sure every student throws the same number of snowballs.
10. Keep score for children or help them keep their own scores.
11. Allow each student to take three turns. Add the total number of points children have for all three turns.
12. Invite students to compare and contrast their total scores. (Examples: Mary Ann has the greatest number of points. Pedro and Natira have the same number of points. Lee has three more points than Ami.) Then have students put their scores in order from least to greatest or greatest to least.

Extension: Assign partners, or allow students to pick their own. Give each pair of students a beanbag or aluminum foil ball. Tell students to play "snowball" catch using underhand throws.

Activity Cards #4 and #5

Activity Card #4: Ice Skating

Supplies:

- white copier paper, two pieces per student and two pieces for demonstration

WARNING: Allow plenty of space for this activity.

Instructions:

1. Give each student two pieces of copier paper to be "ice skates."
2. Go to a location in the school building that has a smooth floor. Tell students to pretend the floor is a frozen pond or skating rink.
3. Show how to step on two papers and glide or slide along the floor.
4. Discuss safety rules before allowing students to "skate."
5. Assign a leader, and place all other students in a line behind the leader. Be sure all students have the opportunity to be the leader.
6. Allow students to use their papers to skate along the floor.
7. Have students ice skate in a variety of patterns such as lines, circles, and figure 8s.

Activity Card #5: The Life of Frosty Snowman

Supplies:

- Interview with Frosty (page 106)
- Pictures of Frosty's Life (page 107)
- large blue construction paper, one piece per student
- Labels for Frosty's Life, one set per student (page 108)
- white construction paper, one piece per student
- Circle Patterns, one set per student (page 109)
- 4" x 4" (10 cm x 10 cm) white construction paper squares, one per student
- scissors
- glue
- markers

Instructions:

1. Ahead of time, reproduce the Circle Patterns on the white construction paper.
2. When students arrive at the center, read the Interview with Frosty to students and display the Pictures of Frosty's Life.
3. Distribute the other materials (listed above) to students.
4. Help children fold the blue construction paper into fourths.
5. Have students use the following directions to show the four stages of Frosty's life on the blue paper: (A) Cut a snowflake out of the white square to glue in the top left-hand corner. (B) Cut out one white circle to glue in the top right-hand corner. (C) Cut out two white circles to glue in the bottom left-hand corner. (D) Cut out three white circles to glue in the bottom right-hand corner.
6. Ask students to use the markers to add details (eyes, nose, mouth, etc.) to their pictures of Frosty.
7. Have students cut out the Labels for Frosty's Life. Help youngsters glue the labels and numbers in the appropriate boxes of the blue paper.
8. Invite students, one at a time, to tell you about the different stages of Frosty's life.

Award Certificate

Give students the Frosty the Snowman's Special Day Award Certificate after they have completed all five center activities. You may prefer to fill in individual student names ahead of time.

✂ -

Congratulations to _____

for completing the

Frosty the Snowman's Special Day Centers!

Happy Holidays!

_____   _____
Teacher   Date

✂ -

Congratulations to _____

for completing the

Frosty the Snowman's Special Day Centers!

Happy Holidays!

_____   _____
Teacher   Date

Snowman Rock Drawing

Bulletin Board Snowman Pattern

Carrot Nose Patterns

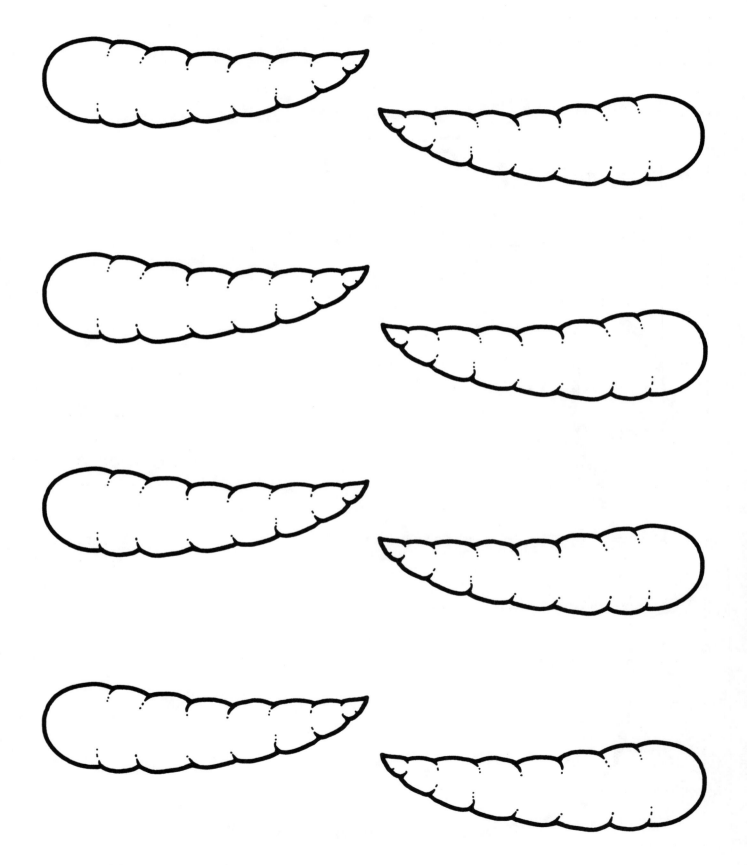

Snowball Toss Scorecards

❄ Snowball Toss Scorecard ❄

Name: _____

Points for Turn #1: _____

Points for Turn #2: _____

Points for Turn #3: _____

Total Number of Points: _____

❄ Snowball Toss Scorecard ❄

Name: _____

Points for Turn #1: _____

Points for Turn #2: _____

Points for Turn #3: _____

Total Number of Points: _____

❄ Snowball Toss Scorecard ❄

Name: _____

Points for Turn #1: _____

Points for Turn #2: _____

Points for Turn #3: _____

Total Number of Points: _____

❄ Snowball Toss Scorecard ❄

Name: _____

Points for Turn #1: _____

Points for Turn #2: _____

Points for Turn #3: _____

Total Number of Points: _____

Interview with Frosty

1. **What is your name?** My name is Frosty the Snowman.
2. **When were you born?** I was born many winters ago.
3. **Where were you born?** I was born in the North Pole, where Santa Claus lives.
4. **Where do you live now?** I move around from place to place. I like to live wherever it snows.
5. **How many people are in your family?** Every snowflake and snowman is part of my family. There are too many to count.
6. **What are your favorite foods?** My favorite foods are snow cones and candy canes.
7. **What do you like to do in your free time?** In my free time, I like to throw snowballs, sing, and dance.
8. **When you were young, what did you like best about school?** I like art lessons, singing, and dance.
9. **What will you do now that you are grown up?** I think I will be a magician since I already have a magic hat.
10. **What are your favorite shows on television?** My favorite TV shows are the holiday specials because many of my friends are in those.

Pictures of Frosty's Life

Baby Frosty

1-year-old Frosty

2-year-old Frosty

Grown-up Frosty

Labels for Frosty's Life

Frosty is a baby.

(snowflake)

Frosty is 1 year old.

(one snowball)

Frosty is 2 years old.

(two snowballs)

Frosty is grown up.

(three snowballs)

| 1 | 2 | 3 | 4 |

Circle Patterns

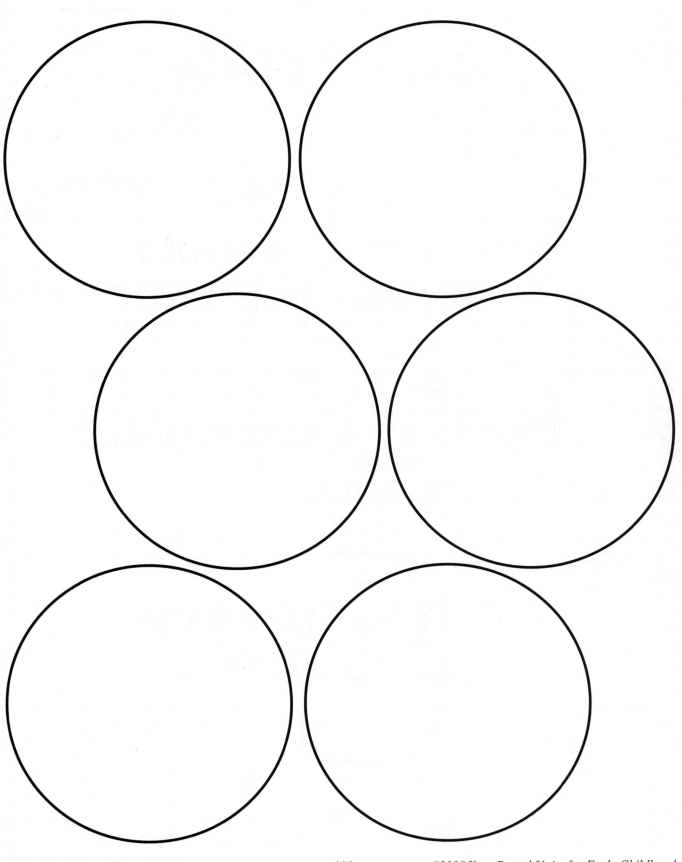

Snack Ideas and Recommended Book

Supplies:

- powdered sugar donut holes, one per student
- large marshmallows, two per student
- toothpicks, two per student
- small tubes of black decorative icing
- fruit roll-ups, one strip per student

- knife (for adult use only)
- small marshmallows, two per student
- small paper plates, one per student
- milk or juice (optional)
- small plastic or paper cups, one per student

WARNINGS: Be sure to ask parents if their children have any food allergies or dietary restrictions. Tell students to be sure to remove the toothpicks before they eat the snowman snack.

Instructions:

Ahead of time, cut the fruit roll-ups into strips so they look like winter scarves.

After students have completed the activities at all five centers, give each child a plate with a donut hole, two large marshmallows, two toothpicks, a fruit roll-up strip, and two small marshmallows. Tell students to pretend that the donut holes are snowballs. Allow students to eat their "snowballs." You may wish to serve cups of milk or juice for students to drink with their snacks.

Then have students use the other ingredients to build a snowman snack. Have students stack the two large marshmallows, one on top of the other. Explain that the top marshmallow will be the snowman's head and the bottom marshmallow will be the snowman's body. You may wish to put a bit of icing between the two marshmallows to help keep them together. Have students wrap the fruit roll-up strip where the snowman's head and body meet. Then have youngsters stick the toothpicks in on opposite sides of the snowman's body. Tell students to put a small marshmallow on the ends of the toothpicks. Help students use the black frosting to add two eyes, a nose, a mouth, and buttons on the snowman. Students will probably have as much fun making these snacks as eating them.

large marshmallows (head and body)

black icing (eyes, nose, mouth, buttons)

fruit roll-up strip (scarf)

toothpicks (arms)

small marshmallows (hands)

Recommended Book: On Frosty the Snowman's Special Day, read aloud *The Biggest, Best Snowman* written by Margery Cuyler (Scholastic, 1998).

Christmas Whole Class Activity

Supplies:

- *Christmas Tree Farm* by Sandra Jordan (Orchard Books, 1996)
- Christmas Tree Sequence Cards (page 112), one set per student
- sentence strips, one per student
- scissors
- glue
- chalkboard
- black fine-tip markers, one per student
- crayons
- pine tree seedlings, one per student (optional)

Instructions:

Read aloud the storybook *Christmas Tree Farm* and discuss it with students. This particular book has an excellent storyline that explains how Christmas trees are grown and harvested.

Give each student a set of Christmas Tree Sequence Cards and a sentence strip. Tell students to sequence the pictures according to what happens first, second, third, and fourth in the life of a Christmas tree. Check to be sure students have placed their pictures in the correct order. Then have students glue the pictures, in order, onto the sentence strip.

Write the numbers 1, 2, 3, and 4 on the chalkboard. Review these numbers with students. Ask students to use a black marker to number their pictures. Invite students to color their pictures.

Visit a local nursery to ask if the owners would like to donate a pine tree seedling for each student in your class. As an alternative, you may wish to request school funds or solicit parent or community donations to pay for the seedlings. Check your school district and local campus policies before asking for donations. Another option is to purchase one pine tree seedling and have students help you plant it in the schoolyard.

If you are able to obtain seedlings for your class, send them home with students. You may wish to include a note that tells parents how to plant and care for the seedlings.

Encourage students to take home the sentence strip with their Christmas Tree Sequence Cards.

Christmas Tree Sequence Cards

Name: _____ Date: _____

tree wrapped in twine

decorated Christmas tree

pine tree seedling

tree haircut (before and after)

Buddy Time Activities

Santa Letters

Have the big buddies help the little buddies write letters to Santa on special stationery (pages 114 and 115). On a chart tablet, write the list (below) of important points that little buddies should include in the Santa letter. Review this list with the big buddies. Display the list while the buddies are working on the letters.

- little buddy's name
- little buddy's grade in school
- ways the little buddy has been good (Examples: cleaning room, sharing toys)
- special presents the little buddy might want from Santa
- a sentence about leaving goodies for Santa and his reindeer
- any questions the little buddy might want to ask Santa

After the buddies write the letter, they should color the Santa picture and glue the beard onto Santa's chin. Have the buddies give the letters to you for mailing to the North Pole. You may wish to arrange for English class students at a nearby junior high or middle school to respond to the buddies' Santa letters. Ask the junior high or middle school teacher to have the older students pretend they are Santa's elves and answer each letter. Be sure that you get the responses to the Santa letters before the buddies leave for the winter holiday. Read aloud the letters from Santa's elves. It is a magical time for youngsters because each letter is so personal.

Christmas Stockings

Ahead of time, reproduce Christmas Stocking Pattern (page 116) on red construction paper, making two stockings per little buddy. Hold two stockings together so that the edges match up. Note that the front will have a decorative border at the top, but the back will not. Punch holes around the edges as indicated on the patterns. Do not punch holes along the top. You may wish to use paperclips to hold each pair of stockings together. Distribute the stockings. Reproduce the Christmas Stocking Decorations (page 117) on white construction paper. Have the little buddies write their names on the decorative label, color it, and glue it onto their stockings. Have the little buddies choose other decorations to color and glue onto their stockings. If youngsters prefer, they can create their own decorations.

Before inviting the big buddies to join your class, cut long pieces of green or white yarn, one per little buddy. Wrap a small piece of masking tape around one end of each piece of yarn to make a "sewing needle." Distribute the pieces of yarn to the little buddies. Tie the end of the yarn without tape onto a top hole of the pair of stockings. Invite the big buddies to help their little buddies sew the Christmas stockings together using the yarn.

At the end of this activity, you may wish to give all the big buddies a small candy cane for a special treat. Give the little buddies a candy cane to put in their stockings. Tell the little buddies that they will be able to eat their candy canes later.

WARNING: Be sure to ask parents if their children have any food allergies or dietary restrictions before allowing students to eat candy canes.

Santa Stationery

(Attach beard here.)

Santa Stationery *(cont.)*

Dear Santa,

_____

_____

_____

_____

_____

_____

Your Friend,

Christmas Stocking Pattern

Trace and cut out two stockings. Hold the stockings together, and punch holes around the edge. Use yarn to sew the stockings together.

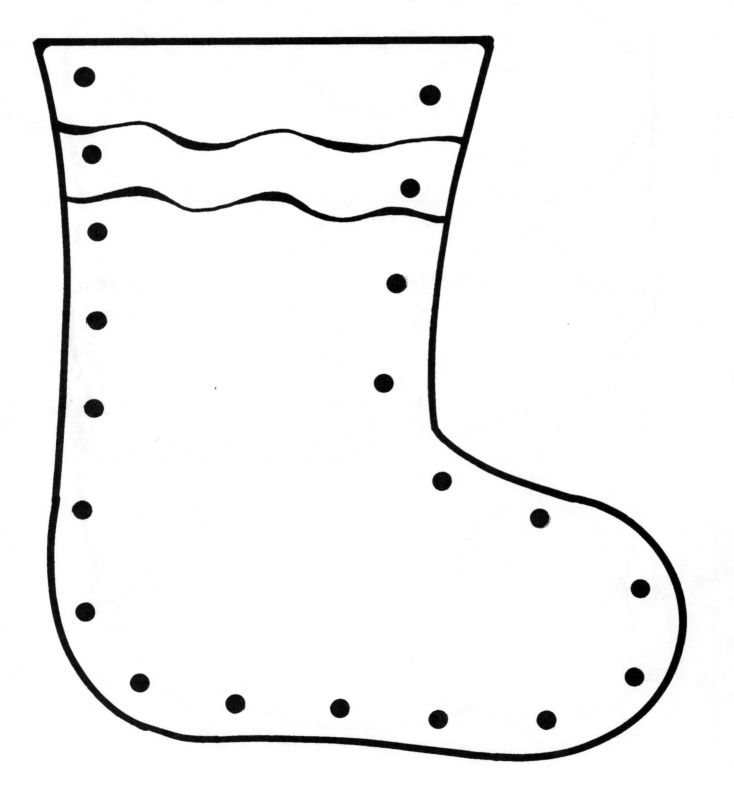

Christmas Stocking Decorations

Elf Backpack Buddy

December Theme: Christmas

Backpack Buddy: small elf doll

Storybook: *The Littlest Christmas Elf* by Nancy Buss (Western Publishing Company, 1995)

Supplies:
- journal
- Letter from Elf Backpack Buddy (page 119)
- Journal Assignment, one per student (page 120)
- backpack
- Elf Backpack Buddy

Instructions:

You may wish to make the writing journals from portfolios with fasteners. Be sure there are enough journal pages (copies of page 120) for every student in the classroom to complete the writing assignment. Inside the journal, also place a copy of the Letter from Elf Backpack Buddy. The homework assignment is described for parents and students in this letter. However, you may prefer to explain the assignment to students before they take it home.

For this journal assignment, students read the book *The Littlest Christmas Elf.* Then they pretend the little elf doll comes to life and plays cute tricks on them while spending the night. Students write about the tricks that the elf plays on them. In the morning, the elf leaves one special present for students. On the bottom half of the writing assignment, there is space for students to draw a picture of this present.

Before sending the backpack home with a different child each day, check to be sure it has the small elf doll, the book *The Littlest Christmas Elf,* and the writing journal. Remind the student who is taking these materials home to return the backpack and its contents the next school day. When it is the next school day, allow time for the student who took the backpack home to share his/her journal writing assignment with the class.

Be sure every student has an opportunity to take the backpack home. After all students have completed the writing assignment, make the journal a permanent addition to your classroom library.

Letter from Elf Backpack Buddy

Hi!

I am Santa's littlest elf, and I love to play cute tricks on people. I can't help it! It's just a part of what elves do. I've included my own special storybook, *The Littlest Christmas Elf,* for you and your parents to read together. I hope you like the book.

After you read the book, please use a page in this journal to write down some of the tricks I play on you and your family tonight. I am not a mean elf, so I only play funny tricks on people. I just like to have a good time.

Since I am an elf, I also like to surprise people by making presents for them. At the bottom of your journal page, you will see a big box. Please draw a special present inside this box. Draw something you would like me to make for — guess who? You!

Thanks for letting me be your Backpack Buddy this month!

Love,

The Littlest Elf

P.S. Please put the book *The Littlest Christmas Elf,* this journal, and me inside the backpack and return all these things to your teacher. That way I can go home with other friends and play tricks on them, too. Thanks!

Journal Assignment

Name: _____ Date: _____

The littlest elf was so cute and funny. The only problem is he has difficulty going to sleep. So while I was sleeping, he played these tricks on my family and me.

_____

_____

_____

_____

_____

_____

_____

When I woke up the next morning, he left this special present in a giant box just for me. It was a _____ .

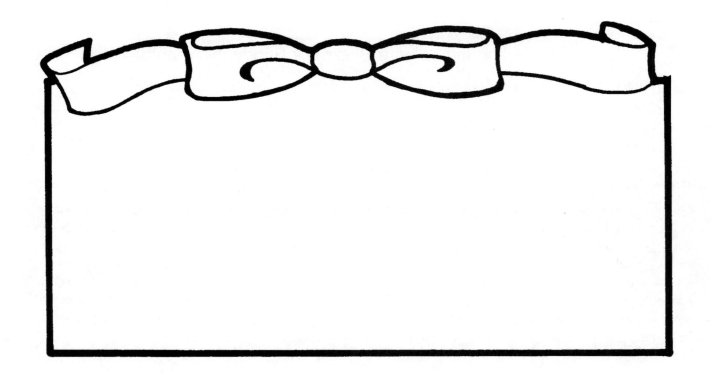

Art & Poetry Activities

Chubby Little Snowman

Supplies:

- large piece of navy blue construction paper, one per student
- Snowman and Bunny Patterns, one per student (page 123)
- "Chubby Little Snowman" poem and "December" title, one per student (top half of page 122)

- white construction paper
- black markers
- scissors
- glue
- white chalk, one piece per student
- Favorite Memories, one per student (page 37)

Instructions:

Ahead of time, reproduce the Snowman and Bunny Patterns on white construction paper. Distribute the blue construction paper, the top half of page 122, and Snowman and Bunny Patterns to students. Read aloud the poem to students. Ask students to cut out the poem and glue it on one half of the blue paper. Tell students to cut out the three circles and carrot from the pattern page. On the other half of the blue paper, have students make a snowman by gluing the circles—one on top of the other, with the largest circle on the bottom and the smallest circle on top. Encourage children to use the black markers to add details, such as eyes, a mouth, buttons, arms, boots, a scarf, and a hat, to the snowman. Have them glue the carrot on as the snowman's nose. Tell students to draw small snowflakes on the blue paper with the white chalk. Ask students to cut out bunny pattern, color it, and glue it on the blue construction paper next to the snowman. Help students complete the Favorite Memories activity sheet. Then have students glue it onto the back of the construction paper.

Christmas Mouse

Supplies:

- Christmas Mouse and Santa's Hat Patterns (page 124)
- "Christmas Mouse" poem and "December" title, one per student (bottom half of page 122)
- large piece of green construction paper, one per student

- cotton balls
- scissors
- glue
- crayons
- Favorite Memories, one per student (page 37)

Instructions:

Give each student a piece of green construction paper, a copy of the patterns, and a copy of the bottom half of page 122. Read aloud the poem "Christmas Mouse" to the class. Have students cut out the poem and glue it on one half of the green paper. Ask students to cut out and color the Santa hat and mouse. Help them cut a slit in the rim of the hat where indicated. Show students how to slide the mouse into the slit of the hat. Then tell students to glue the mouse and hat onto the blank half of the green paper. Have children glue the "December" title to the top of the green paper and cotton balls to the top and rim of the hat and. If students have not already done a Favorite Memories activity sheet, help them complete one now. Tell them to glue it onto the back of this artwork.

December Poems

Chubby Little Snowman

(Author Unknown)

A chubby little snowman had a carrot for a nose,

Along came a bunny and what do you suppose?

That hungry little bunny was looking for his lunch.

He ate that little snowman's nose…nibble, nibble, crunch!

December

Christmas Mouse

I'm the little Christmas mouse

Who climbs up your tree.

I'm the little Christmas mouse

Who nibbles on your cheese.

I'm the little Christmas mouse

Who teases the cat.

I'm the little Christmas mouse

Asleep in Santa's hat!

Shhhhhhh!

December

Snowman and Bunny Patterns

Christmas Mouse and Santa's Hat Patterns

Thematic Pins & Magnets

A snowman magnet or pin is the perfect gift for the month of December. By gluing a student's photograph next to the snowman, this craft becomes a unique personalized holiday present. Other holiday patterns are included below and on page 126 so students can choose to make their favorites. You may wish to use the larger patterns (page 126) with younger students, since these patterns are easier for little hands to work with, and the smaller patterns (below) for older students, adult helpers, and yourself.

Instructions for the snowman pin or magnet are given below. Additional directions, as well as other ideas for materials to use when creating these gifts, are provided on page 9 of the How to Use Thematic Teaching Ideas section of this book.

Supplies:

- snowman pattern (below)
- full-body photograph of each student
- white chalk
- tacky glue

- textured white vinyl
- black felt
- black and red fabric paint
- magnetic strip or pin, one per pattern
- scissors

Instructions:

1. Have students trace the snowman pattern on to the white vinyl.
2. Tell students to cut out the vinyl snowman. Provide cutting assistance as needed.
3. Use white chalk to trace the hat and boot patterns on the black felt. Make one set for each child, or allow students to trace the patterns themselves.
4. Ask students to cut out the black felt hat and boots. Provide cutting assistance as needed.
5. Have students use the black fabric paint to add the eyes, mouth, arms, and buttons to the snowman and the red fabric paint to add the nose, scarf, and mittens to the snowman.
6. On the long white section next to each vinyl snowman, glue a student's photograph.
7. Help students glue a magnetic strip or pin onto the back of the snowman and student's photograph.

December Patterns

Christmas Videotaping Ideas

The general directions for how to make a Class Video Book are on page 10 of the How to Use Thematic Teaching Ideas section of this book.

Before videotaping, reproduce the Antler Headband (page 128), one per student, on brown construction paper. Give each student a headband to cut out. Then give children paintbrushes and some green and red tempera paint. Tell them to paint the holly leaves green and the berries red. Allow the paint to dry. Cut 20" x 2" (50 cm x 5 cm) tagboard strips, one per student. To make each headband, wrap a tagboard strip so it fits comfortably around a child's head. Carefully remove the headband from the child's head without changing the size. Staple the ends in place. Then staple the youngster's antlers onto the tagboard headband. Give the completed headband to the student to wear for the videotaping.

You may wish to ask students if they would like to have their noses painted red. Use red water-base paint for this. Students who do not feel comfortable having their noses painted do not need to do so.

Allow time for students to learn and practice the song "Rudolph the Red-Nosed Reindeer" (below).

To begin the December videotaping, use a Rudolph or reindeer stuffed toy to introduce the new reindeer (your students). Then have Rudolph explain that his reindeer friends will be singing his favorite holiday song, "Rudolph the Red-Nosed Reindeer." Then videotape the students singing the traditional version of "Rudolph the Red-Nosed Reindeer." After finishing the song, zoom the camera in on students, one at a time, so they can wish their families a Merry Christmas, Happy Hanukkah, or Happy Holiday. You may wish to invite students to say the names of their family members as part of the video. At the end of the December videotaping segment, encourage students to look at the camera, wave, and say all together, *Happy Holidays, Mom and Dad!*

Rudolph the Red-Nosed Reindeer
(Traditional)

Rudolph the red-nosed reindeer

Had a very shiny nose

And if you ever saw it,

You would even say it glows.

All of the other reindeer

Use to laugh and call him names.

They never let poor Rudolph

Join in any reindeer games.

Then one foggy Christmas Eve

Santa came to say,

"Rudolph, with your nose so bright,

Won't you guide my sleigh tonight?"

Then how the reindeer loved him

As they shouted out with glee,

"Rudolph the red-nosed reindeer,

You'll go down in history!"

Antler Headband

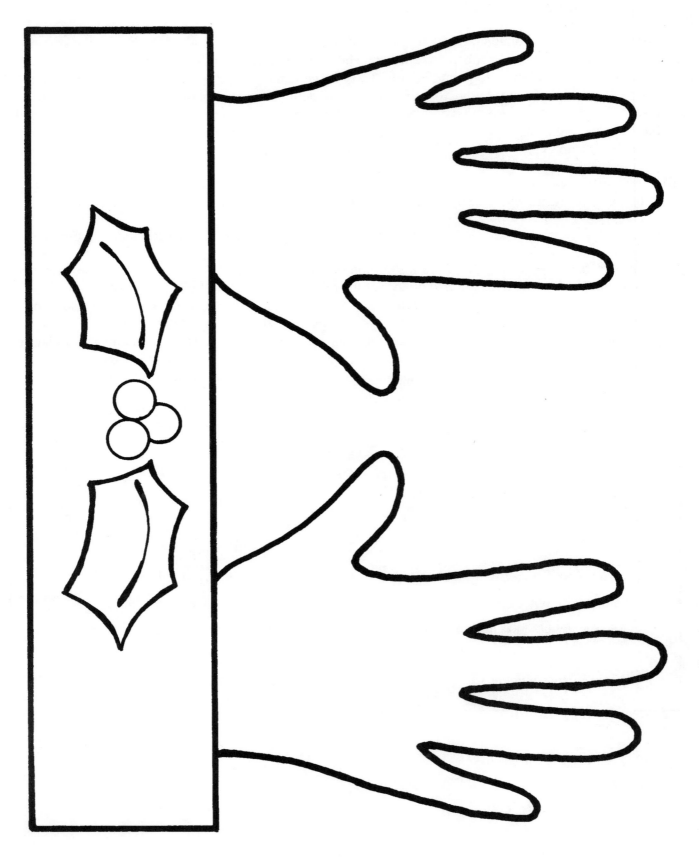

January Themes: Sea Life and New Year's Day

Section Contents

Bibliography

Hopkins, T. *1001 Best Web Sites for Educators.* Teacher Created Materials, 2000. URL updates are available at the following address: http://www.teachercreated.com

Sea Life

Clements, Andrew. *Big Al.* Simon & Schuster Children's, 1997.

Dolphin Adventures. Videotape. Audubon's Animal Adventures, 1997. 30 minutes.

Faulkner, Keith. *The Runaway Whale.* Borders Press, 1992.

Hirschi, Ron. *Discover My World (Whales and Other Sea Creatures).* Bantam Books, 1991.

Lester, Helen. *Three Cheers for Tacky.* Houghton Mifflin, 1996.

Lionni, Leo. *Swimmy.* Knopf, 1991.

Milton, Joyce. *Whales, the Gentle Giants* (Step 2). Random House, 1989.

Pfister, Marcus. *The Rainbow Fish.* North South Books, 1992.

Pfister, Marcus. *Rainbow Fish to the Rescue!* North South Books, 1988.

Sheldon, Dyan. *The Whales' Song.* Viking Penguin, 1997.

Whale Adventures. Videotape. Audubon's Animal Adventures, 1997. 30 minutes.

http://www.seaworld.org/ask-shamu/asindex.html This Web site contains answers to questions about many sea creatures' lives and habitats.

New Year's Day

Carrier, Roch. *A Happy New Year's Day.* Tundra Books, 1994.

Gill, Janie Spaht. *New Year's (Holiday Books).* ARO, 1997.

Reese, Nancy. *New Year's (Holiday Books).* ARO, 1997.

Activity Cards #1 and #2

Activity Card #1: Objects that Float or Sink

Supplies:

- Float or Sink?, one per group or one per student (page 134)
- container such as a large pan, bowl, or washtub
- water
- objects — small seashell, craft stick, cotton ball, pebble, toothpick, small rubber whale, rubber band, pencil, crayon, eraser, table tennis ball, paper clip, modeling clay, drinking straw, penny

Instructions:

1. Ahead of time, pour water into the container until it is half full.
2. Position students' seating so they can all see into the container of water.
3. Have students predict whether each object will sink or float before you put it in the water.
4. Then have students take turns dropping the objects (listed above) into the water to discover which ones will float and which ones will sink.
5. Record the answers for students on the Float or Sink? chart, or have students record the answers on individual copies of the chart.
6. Discuss with students why some objects float, while others sink.

Extension: Collect other objects for students to conduct additional float or sink experiments.

Activity Card #2: Whale Strings and PE Games

Supplies:

- one piece of blue yarn, 100 feet (30 cm) in length
- one piece of red yarn, 65 feet (19.5 cm) in length
- one piece of yellow yarn, 25 feet (7.5 cm) in length
- wide masking tape or duct tape
- Graph Patterns (pages 137 and 138, optional)

Instructions:

1. After you have cut the yarn to the lengths specified above, stretch out the three pieces along the ground so they are parallel and about 3 feet (0.9 m) apart from each other. Use wide masking tape or duct tape to secure the ends of each piece of yarn to the ground.
2. Tell students that the three pieces of yarn represent the lengths of three different types of whales. The blue yarn represents the length of the blue whale, the red yarn represents the length of the humpback whale, and the yellow yarn represents the length of the Orca, or killer whale. You may wish to show pictures of these three whales using the Graph Patterns provided for Activity Card #5 page 132.
3. Ask students to compare and contrast the sizes of these whales using the pieces of yarn. Example: The blue whale is longer than the humpback whale.
4. Have students do different movements as they move up and down the pieces of yarn. For example, students could scissor-walk, tiptoe, run, walk backwards, hop, crawl, etc., the length of each whale.

Activity Cards #3 and #4

Activity Card #3: Big Al Booklet

Supplies:

- *Big Al* by Andrew Clements (Simon & Schuster Children's, 1997)
- Big Al Booklet (page 135)
- crayons
- markers
- scissors
- stapler and staples

Instructions:

1. Read aloud the book *Big Al* by Andrew Clements.
2. Discuss with students why it was so difficult for Big Al to make friends and how the other fish knew Al was really a very kind fish.
3. Distribute the Big Al Booklet to students. Read aloud the booklet. Point out that the events in the booklet are in the same order as the events in the book.
4. Ask youngsters to color the pictures and cut apart the booklet pages.
5. Help students put the booklet pages in the correct order. Then staple the pages along the left-hand side for students.
6. Have students write their names on the cover. If time allows, reread the booklet with students. Encourage youngsters to take their booklets home to share with their families.

Extension: Prepare small booklets with blank paper in them for students to write and illustrate their own sea life stories.

Activity Card #4: Whale Addition

Supplies:

- number cubes, one per student
- Whale Addition, one per student (page 136)
- pencils or crayons
- counting manipulatives, twelve per student (optional)

Instructions:

1. Give each student a number cube and a copy of the Whale Addition activity sheet.
2. Show students how to roll the cube and read the number at the top.
3. Tell students to roll the number cube two times and record the numbers in the first and second blanks of a whale on the activity sheet.
4. Have students add the two numbers they rolled to get the sum. Depending on the ability level of students, you may wish to provide manipulatives for students to use when adding.
5. Tell them to write the sum in the blank on the whale's tail.
6. Have students follow the same procedure for the other three whales on the activity sheet.
7. After students have completed the four math problems, teach students how to read aloud an addition problem. Example: If the problem reads $4 + 2 = 6$, you should say, "Four plus two equals six."
8. Invite children to share their addition problems with the group.

Activity Card #5

Activity Card #5: My Favorite Whale and Dolphin Graph

Supplies:

- Graph Patterns (pages 137 and 138)
- scissors
- tape
- yarn
- small or medium-sized sticky notes, one per student
- pencils

Instructions:

1. On a wall, create the lines of a graph using yarn. Use the Graph Patterns to label the graph as shown.

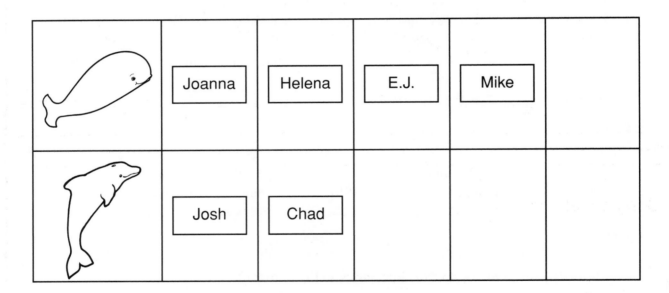

2. Ask students to decide which animal (whale or dolphin) shown on the graph is their favorite.

3. Give each student a sticky note. Ask students to write their names on the sticky note and place it on the graph, next to the animal that is their favorite.

4. Discuss the graph with students. Ask students to read and interpret the data represented by the graph. Sample questions: *How many votes did the humpback whale get? Which animal had the most votes? Which animal had the least votes? How many votes did the dolphin and killer whale get altogether?*

Extension: Collect a variety of whale books for students to enjoy.

Award Certificate

Give students the Sea Life's Special Day Award Certificate after they have completed all five center activities. You may prefer to fill in individual student names ahead of time.

✂ -

Congratulations to _____

for completing the

Sea Life's Special Day Centers!

_____   _____
Teacher   Date

✂ -

Congratulations to _____

for completing the

Sea Life's Special Day Centers!

_____   _____
Teacher   Date

Float or Sink?

Name: _____ Date: _____

Write a check mark (✓) in the correct column to show whether each object floats or sinks.

Objects	Floats	Sinks
1. seashell		
2. craft stick		
3. cotton ball		
4. pebble		
5. toothpick		
6. small rubber whale		
7. rubber band		
8. pencil		
9. crayon		
10. eraser		
11. table tennis ball		
12. paper clip		
13. modeling clay		
14. drinking straw		
15. penny		

Big Al Booklet

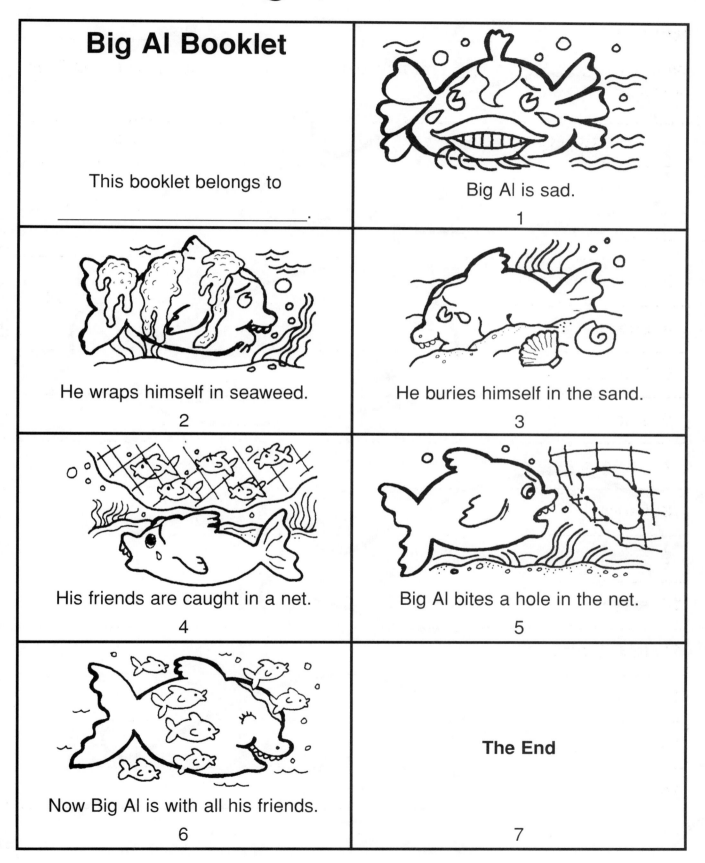

Big Al Booklet

This booklet belongs to

_____.

Big Al is sad.

1

He wraps himself in seaweed.

2

He buries himself in the sand.

3

His friends are caught in a net.

4

Big Al bites a hole in the net.

5

Now Big Al is with all his friends.

6

The End

7

Whale Addition

Name: _____ Date: _____

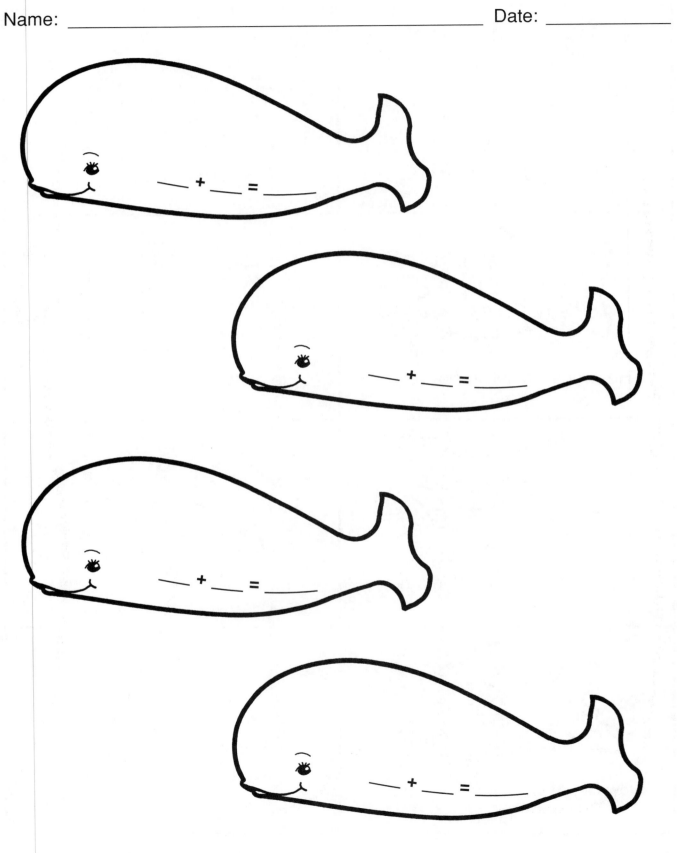

Graph Patterns

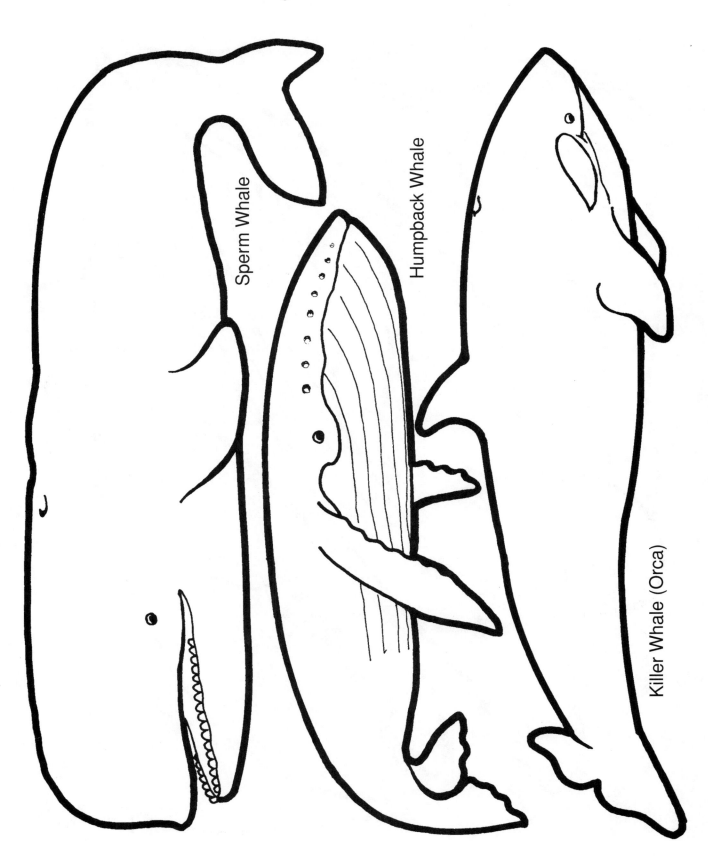

Sperm Whale

Humpback Whale

Killer Whale (Orca)

Graph Patterns *(cont.)*

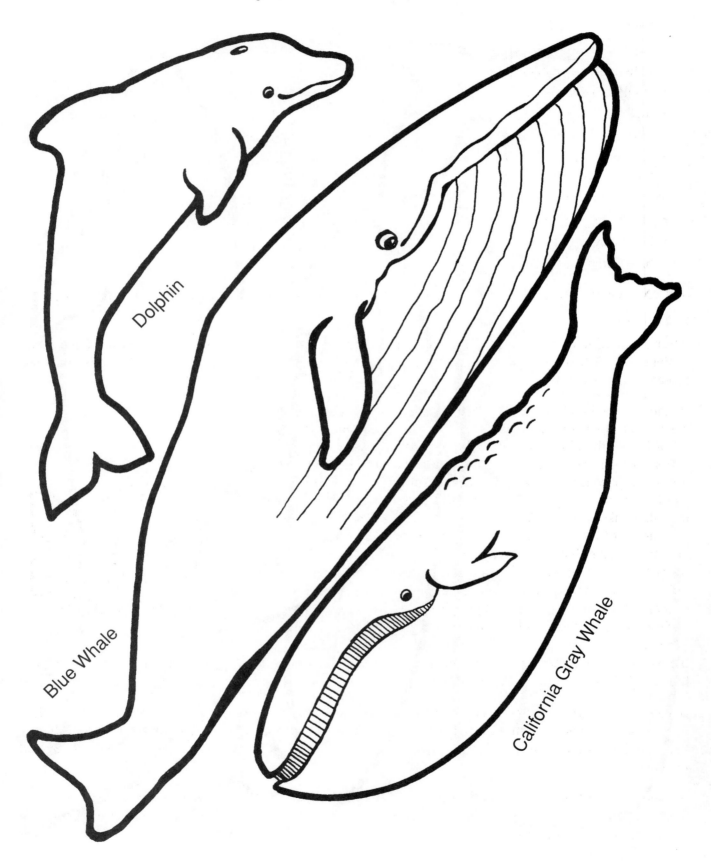

Snack Ideas and Recommended Book

Supplies:

- paper cups, two per student
- fish-shaped crackers
- small marshmallows
- juice
- cake mix
- cake mix ingredients and cooking tools, as listed on the package
- two round cake pans
- knife (for adult use only)
- large tray
- blue butcher paper

- canned white frosting
- plastic or Styrofoam bowls
- food coloring
- candy-coated chocolates
- cupcake tins (optional)
- chocolate frosting (optional)
- seashells (optional)
- green tissue paper (optional)
- paper plates, one per student
- plastic forks, one per student

WARNING: Be sure to ask parents if their children have any food allergies or dietary restrictions.

Instructions:

After completion of all five sea life centers, invite students to enjoy a special sea life snack. Give each student some fish-shaped crackers and small marshmallows in a cup. Tell students that the marshmallows represent the fish eggs.

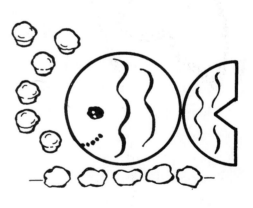

In addition to the above snack idea, you may wish to make a cake in the shape of a fish. To do this, prepare the cake mix according to the directions on the back of the package. Pour the batter into the two round cake pans. Bake the cake. Then allow it to cool thoroughly. Take the cakes out of the pans. Place one whole cake on a large tray covered with blue butcher paper. Cut the other cake in half. From one half, cut a triangle shape out of the middle of the flat side. Place the rounded side of this half next to the cake that has not been cut. The whole round cake is the fish's body and the half with the triangle cut out is the fish's tail. Separate the frosting into several bowls. Add food coloring to make different colored frostings. Frost the fish with the different colors. Use candy-coated chocolates to make the fish's eye and mouth. Cut the left-over cake half into three or four pieces to look like rocks. Use chocolate icing on these and place them under the fish cake so the fish looks as if it is swimming above the rocks.

If you have a large class and need more cake, in addition to making the cake as described above, make cupcakes. Use blue frosting (white frosting with blue food coloring) on these to make them look like fish bubbles. You may wish to add some real seashells and twisted green tissue paper (seaweed) around the cake.

Recommended Book: On Sea Life's Special Day, read aloud *The Whale's Song* written by Dyan Sheldon with paintings by Gary Blythe (Viking Penguin, 1997). This story has a wonderful message about the beautiful humpback whales.

New Year's Whole Class Activity

Supplies:

- Children's Book: *A Happy New Year's Day* by Roch Carrier (Tundra Books of Northern New York, 1994)
- Hot Air Balloon Pattern (page 141)
- blank transparency
- overhead projector
- butcher paper
- markers
- glue
- full-body photograph of each student

Instructions:

Cover a bulletin board with butcher paper. Make a transparency of the Hot Air Balloon Pattern. Use an overhead projector and markers to enlarge the pattern and trace it onto the butcher paper. Be sure to include the words "Happy New Year!" on the balloon.

Read aloud the storybook *A Happy New Year's Day* and discuss it with students. Invite youngsters to share some of their ideas about how their parents or family members celebrate New Year's Eve and New Year's Day.

Carefully cut out students' photographs and place them in the hot air balloon basket so it looks like they are passengers. Depending on the skill level of your students, children may be able to cut out and glue the photographs. You may wish to write on the basket, *Here's to the year _____!* (insert the year)

Ask students, one at a time, to go up to the bulletin board and draw something they might see at a party and write a slogan or expression they might hear at a party.

Drawings may include the following:

- cakes
- horns
- party hats
- party streamers
- people dancing
- musical notes
- balloons

Slogans/expressions may include the following:

- Let's celebrate!
- We made it to the year _____!
- Whoopee! Party Time!

Extension: Have students write personal New Year's goals on writing paper. After students have written their goals, cut around the writing paper so that each piece looks like a cloud. Attach these to the bulletin board around the hot air balloon.

Hot Air Balloon Pattern

Happy New Year!

Buddy Time Activities

New Year's Goals

Reproduce a class set of the New Year's Goals (page 143). You may wish to reproduce two sets so the big buddies and little buddies can each have a goal sheet of their own. Ask the big buddies to interview the little buddies, using the sentence starters on the activity sheet. Have the buddies work together to draw pictures that go with their goals for the New Year. Make a class book by stapling the activity pages between two pieces of construction paper. Write the title *Our New Year's Goals* on the front cover. Encourage children to share the book with their parents at conferences or other school events. As an alternative, allow students to check the book out for a couple of days so they can take it home to share with their families.

Sea Creatures

Reproduce the Sea Creature Stories (page 144), making one copy for every two pairs of buddies. Cut the copies in half along the dotted line. Then glue each half-page onto the back of a large piece of white construction paper. Allow the glue to dry.

You may wish to begin this activity by asking the buddies to brainstorm the names of sea creatures. Write students' suggestions on the chalkboard. Youngsters may refer to this list as they work on the Sea Creature Stories. Point out that the creatures the buddies write about can be real or imaginary.

Then distribute the white construction paper with the activity sheets glued on the back to each pair of buddies. Ask the big buddies and little buddies to work together to fill out the Sea Creature Stories. Encourage students to color a picture of their sea creatures on the blank side of the construction paper.

Allow time for the buddies to share their stories and artwork.

Something to Spout About

To help build self-esteem, have the big buddies help their little buddies fill out the Something to Spout About Form (page 145). On butcher paper, draw a large whale or enlarge the whale pattern provided on page 151. Attach the whale to the center of a bulletin board. It should be close to the bottom. Staple blue yarn to the bulletin board so it looks like water is coming out of the whale's blowhole. Use blue butcher paper to make a wave pattern under the whale. Attach students' completed forms around the whale. Use large letters to add the title *Something to Spout About*.

New Year's Goals

Little Buddy's Name: _____

Big Buddy's Name: _____

Date: _____

Some places I would really like to go this year are _____

_____ .

A friend I would like to visit is _____ .

Some famous holiday characters are the Easter Bunny, a leprechaun, Santa Claus, and a ghost. A famous holiday character I would like to meet is

_____ .

Some things I would like to learn how to do are _____ .

A new toy I would like to get this year is _____ .

I would like to go out to eat with my parents at _____ .

In the box below, draw a picture to show one of the goals you wrote about above.

Happy New Year!

Sea Creature Stories

Our Sea Creature

Little Buddy's Name: _____

Big Buddy's Name: _____

Date: _____

Our sea creature's name is _____ .

Our sea creature likes to _____

_____ .

Its favorite food is _____

_____ .

We like our sea creature because _____

_____ .

✂ -

Our Sea Creature

Little Buddy's Name: _____

Big Buddy's Name: _____

Date: _____

Our sea creature's name is _____ .

Our sea creature likes to _____

_____ .

Its favorite food is _____

_____ .

We like our sea creature because _____

_____ .

Something to Spout About

Little Buddy's Name: _____

Big Buddy's Name: _____

Date: _____

Here are some things I can do well:

1. _____

2. _____

3. _____

Here's a picture of me doing something I can do well:

Here are some things I would like to learn to do better:

1. _____

2. _____

3. _____

Penguin Backpack Buddy

January Theme: Sea Life

Backpack Buddy: small stuffed penguin

Storybook: *Three Cheers for Tacky* written by Helen Lester and illustrated by Lynn Munsinger (Houghton Mifflin Company, 1996)

Supplies:
- journal
- Letter from Penguin Backpack Buddy (page 147)
- Journal Assignment, one per student (page 148)
- backpack
- Penguin Backpack Buddy

Instructions:

You may wish to make the writing journals from portfolios with fasteners. Be sure there are enough journal pages (copies of page 148) for every student in the classroom to complete the writing assignment. Also place a copy of the Letter from Penguin Backpack Buddy inside the journal. The homework assignment is described for parents and students in this letter. However, you may prefer to explain the assignment to students before they take it home.

For this journal assignment, students read the book *Three Cheers for Tacky.* Parents and their children discuss the silly cheer Tacky makes up in this story. Then youngsters make up a new rhyming cheer for Tacky. In addition, they draw a picture of Tacky doing the cheer.

Before sending the backpack home with a different child each day, check to be sure it has the small stuffed penguin, the book *Three Cheers for Tacky,* and the writing journal. Remind the student who is taking these materials home to return the backpack and its contents the next school day. When it is the next school day, allow time for the student who took the backpack home to share his/her journal writing assignment with the class.

Be sure every student has an opportunity to take the backpack home. After all students have completed the writing assignment, make the journal a permanent addition to your classroom library.

Letter from Penguin Backpack Buddy

Hi! — Bye! — Hi! — Bye! — Hi! — Bye!

My name is Tacky, and I'm a silly, mixed-up penguin with a big heart. One day, while I was still inside my egg, I rolled down a hill and slightly cracked my shell. Shortly after that, I was born. I've always been a little different than other penguins. You can read more about me in Helen Lester's book *Three Cheers for Tacky.* In the story, I make up a silly cheer, and the audience loves it!

After you read *Three Cheers for Tacky,* please use a page in this journal to make up a new cheer for me. The cheer can be about anything you are interested in and want us to cheer about! Below is an example of a cheer I just made up.

Tacky is so chubby and sweet.

He has the cutest webbed feet!

1 — 2 — 3 and 4.

There he waddles through my door!

When you are done writing your cheer, draw a picture of me doing your cheer. Have fun!

Hi! — Bye! — Hi! — Bye! — Hi! — Bye!

From,

Tacky the Penguin

P.S. Please don't forget to put the book *Three Cheers for Tacky,* this journal, and me inside the backpack and return all of these things to your teacher. You will get to share your cheer and the picture you drew of me doing your cheer, and another student will get to take me home.

Journal Assignment

Name: _____ Date: _____

Here is my cheer for Tacky.

_____

_____

_____

_____

_____

_____

Here is a picture of Tacky doing my cheer.

Art & Poetry Activities

New Year's Day
Supplies:

- white construction paper, one-half piece per student
- different colors of tempera paint
- straws, one per student
- black construction paper, one piece per student
- glue
- scissors
- "New Year's Day" poem and "January" title, one per student (top half of page 150)
- large piece of construction paper, one per student (any bright color)
- Favorite Memories, one per student (page 37)

Instructions:

Give each student one-half of a piece of white construction paper and a straw. Ask each student to pick colors of tempera paint. Randomly place a few drops of the selected paint colors on each student's white paper. Tell students to gently blow through their straws to spread the paint across the paper, creating a splattered effect. When the paint dries, glue each student's artwork onto a piece of black construction paper. Distribute the top half of page 150 to students. Read aloud the poem. Help children complete the poem. Have students cut out the poem and "January" title. Then help youngsters mount the artwork, poem, and title on a large piece of construction paper. Help students complete the Favorite Memories activity sheet. Ask students to glue it onto the back of the large construction paper.

Beautiful Whales
Supplies:

- blue or green finger-paint
- medium-sized finger-painting paper, one piece per student
- Whale Pattern, one per student (page 151)
- black construction paper, one piece per student
- glue
- medium-sized plastic eyes, one per student
- markers
- large piece of green or light blue construction paper, one per student
- "Beautiful Whales" poem and "January" title, one per student (bottom half of page 150)
- Favorite Memories, one per student (page 37)

Instructions:

Distribute the supplies listed above. Have children use fingerpaints and finger-paint paper to make underwater scenes. Ask youngsters to trace the Whale Pattern on to black construction paper and cut it out. Have students glue the whale to the underwater picture and glue a plastic eye to the whale. Tell children to use the markers to add details to the whale. Read aloud the poem "Beautiful Whales." Have students cut out the poem and the "January" title. Then help youngsters mount the artwork, poem, and title on a large piece of construction paper. If students have not already done a Favorite Memories activity sheet, help them complete one now. Tell them to glue it onto the back of the construction paper.

January Poems

New Year's Day

A whole new year has just begun.

It's time to go and have some fun!

Here are some things I'd like to do:

1. _____

2. _____

3. _____

And make a brand new friend or two!

Happy New Year!

January

Beautiful Whales

Beautiful whales, big and strong,

Growing to over 100 feet long.

Come great whales, and swim by me.

Dip through the waves of the deep blue sea.

January

Whale Pattern

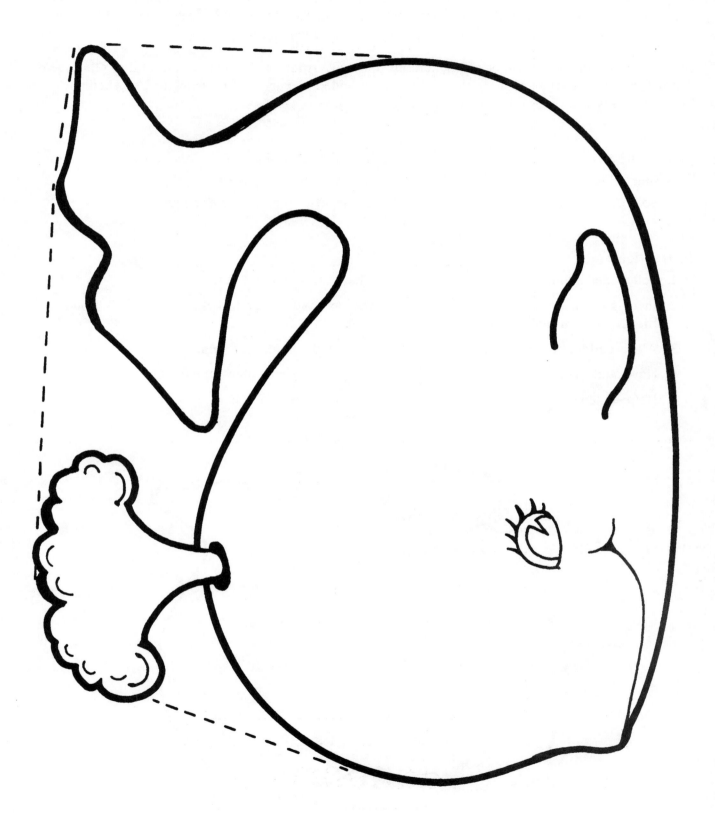

Thematic Pins & Magnets

Whale pins and magnets are the perfect gifts to accompany the sea life unit in this book. Below are simple directions for making the whale gifts. Several other sea life and whales patterns are included below and on page 153. Use the ones that are most appropriate for your students. You may wish to make smaller baby whale pins to accompany larger whale magnet gifts.

Instructions for the whale pin or magnet are given below. Additional directions, as well as other ideas for materials to use when creating these gifts, are provided on page 9 of the How to Use Thematic Teaching Ideas section of this book.

Supplies:

- whale pattern (below)
- blue vinyl
- gold glitter glue
- glue
- white and black liquid embroidery paint
- plastic eyes, one per pattern
- magnetic strip or pin, one per pattern

Instructions:

1. Tell students to trace the whale pattern onto blue vinyl and cut it out.
2. Invite students to use the white and black liquid embroidery paint to draw the whale's mouth, flipper, and tail lines.
3. Allow children to draw extra waterspout lines using the gold glitter glue.
4. Have students glue the plastic eye onto the front of the whale, above the mouth.
5. Help students glue a magnetic strip or pin onto the back of the whale.

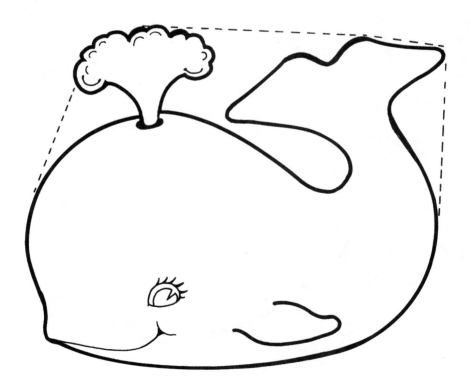

January Patterns

Sea Life Videotaping Ideas

The general directions for how to make a Class Video Book are on page 10 of the How to Use Thematic Teaching Ideas section of this book. Before starting the January videotaping session, make transparencies of the Sea Chant Patterns (pages 156 and 157). Use an overhead projector to enlarge the patterns onto large construction paper or butcher paper. Display the whales and dolphin in the classroom for the videotaping session.

Allow time for students to learn and practice the Sea Chant (page 155). The chant contains specific facts about and characteristics of dolphins and five types of whales. When videotaping, zoom the camera in on the picture of the appropriate whale or dolphin before students say that part of the chant (verses 3–8). Then videotape students reciting that part of the chant. For example, show the picture of the blue whale before students recite verse 3.

To add more rhythm and action when reciting the chant, between each verse have students slap their laps with both hands, while chanting, "Bump-bump, bump-bump, bump-bump, bump-bump!" The last set of bump-bumps should be slower than the first three sets.

You may also wish to have youngsters use their arms and hands to act out the motions described in the chant. Model for students the movements you want. Then have students follow your lead.

You may wish to include the big buddies in this videotaping session. Simply copy the Sea Chant on a piece of tagboard, poster board, or chart paper. As an alternative, you can reproduce the chant on a transparency and display it on a screen using an overhead projector. Allow the big and little buddies to practice reciting the Sea Chant together. When you are done recording the chant, ask the little buddies, one at a time, to introduce their big buddies. Zoom the camera in on the little and big buddies.

To end this videotaping session, have students look at the camera, wave, and say all together, *Happy whale watching, Mom and Dad!*

Sea Chant

Beautiful whales, big and strong,
Growing to over 100 feet long.
Diving and swimming all about,
Breathing through your special blow spout.

Come, great whale,
And swim by me,
Dip through the waves
Of the deep blue sea.

Blue whale, blue whale, gentle and free
With baleen teeth, you won't eat me.
Smooth and beautiful — 100 feet long,
The largest animal — so big and strong.

Dolphin, dolphin, what do you see?
She sees children swimming in the sea.
Flipping and jumping, she loves to play.
A small young dolphin could play all day.

Humpback, humpback, with big white fins,
In the Atlantic Ocean he swims.
Patches is his real name,
Breaching by boats is his favorite game.

Sperm whale, sperm whale, with a toothy grin,
Swimming by and waving a fin.
Way down deep you dive and swish,
Looking for some tasty fish.

Killer whale, killer whale, black and white,
Swimming all day and through the night.
Shamu, your brother, puts on quite a show.
You're the smartest whale I know.

Gray whale, gray whale, 50 feet long,
Singing and whistling a lullaby song.
Traveling south to Mexico's sea,
To the warm, warm waters to have a baby.

Sea Chant Patterns

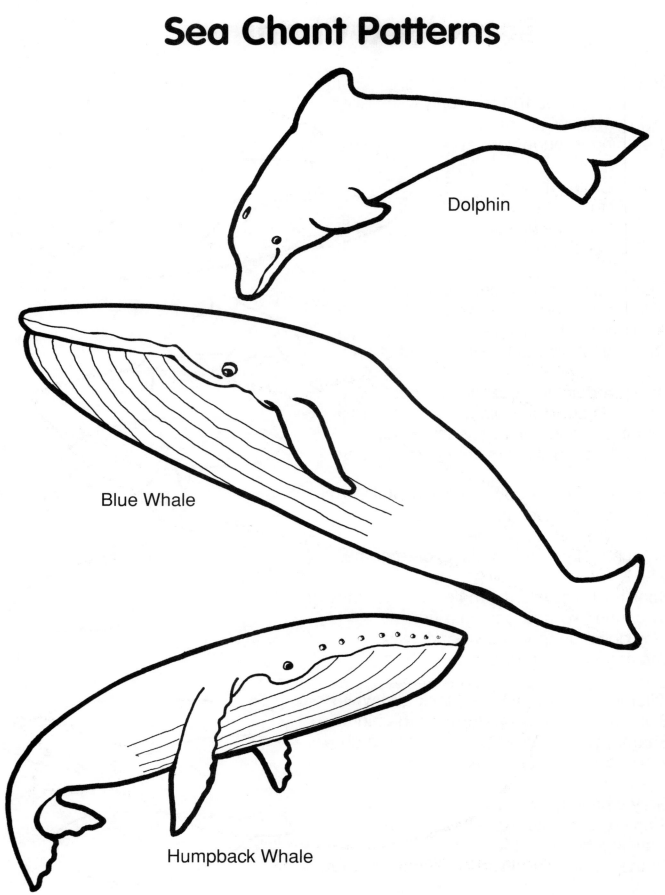

Dolphin

Blue Whale

Humpback Whale

Sea Chant Patterns *(cont.)*

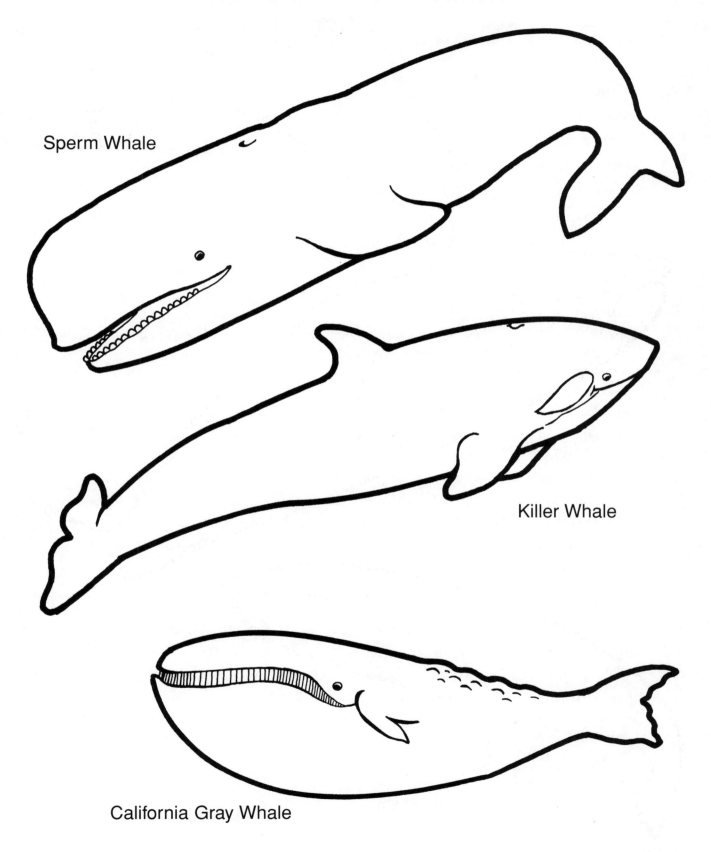

Sperm Whale

Killer Whale

California Gray Whale

February Themes: Valentine's Day and Presidents' Birthdays

Section Contents

Bibliography

Hopkins, T. *1001 Best Web Sites for Educators*. Teacher Created Materials, 2000. URL updates are available at the following address: http://www.teachercreated.com

Valentine's Day

Berenstain, Stan and Jan. *The Berenstain Bears' Comic Valentine*. Scholastic, 1997.

Brandenberg, Aliki. *Feelings*. William Morrow and Company, 1986.

Bridwell, Norman. *Clifford's First Valentine's Day*. Scholastic, 1996.

Hoban, Lillian. *Arthur's Great Big Valentine*. HarperCollins Children's Books, 1990.

Kraus, Robert. *How Spider Saved Valentine's Day*. Scholastic, 1986.

Modesitt, Jeanne. *Sometimes I Feel Like a Mouse*. Scholastic, 1996.

Franklin's Valentines. Videotape. Nelvanu Polygram Video, 1997. 25 minutes.

Presidents' Birthdays

Adler, David A. *A Picture Book of Abraham Lincoln*. Holiday House, 1990.

Adler, David A. *A Picture Book of George Washington*. Holiday House, 1995.

Borden, Louise. *A. Lincoln and Me*. Scholastic, 1999.

Brenner, Martha. *Abe Lincoln's Hat (Step 2 Book)*. Random House, 1994.

Giblin, James Cross. *George Washington: A Picture Book Biography*. Scholastic, 1997.

Activity Cards #1 and #2

Activity Card #1: Heart Animals

Supplies:

- pink, purple, and red construction paper
- large piece of white construction paper one per student
- Heart Animals, one per student (page 163)
- Heart Patterns, one per student (page 164)

- pencil
- scissors
- glue
- markers

Instructions:

1. Ahead of time, trace numerous copies of the Heart Patterns on pink, purple, and red construction paper. Cut out the construction paper hearts and place them on a table.
2. Distribute the copies of Heart Animals and white construction paper to students. Tell children that they can use the hearts to make the animals shown or other types of animals.
3. Ask students to glue pink, purple, and red hearts onto the white construction paper to make some animals.
4. Have students use markers to add details to their heart animals.

Activity Card #2: Heart Envelopes

Supplies:

- large red construction paper, two pieces per student
- Heart Pillow Pattern (page 166, optional)
- long strands of white, pink, or blue yarn, one piece per student

- heart stickers
- glitter glue or white liquid embroidery paint

Instructions:

1. Ahead of time, place two pieces of large red construction paper together. Fold them in half and cut out a heart shape from both pieces of paper at the same time. Continue in this manner until you have two identical paper hearts for each student. If you prefer to use a pattern, there is one provided for Activity Card #4 (Heart Pillow Pattern, page 166) that will work well.
2. Hold each pair of hearts together and punch holes around the edge, except at the top. Space the holes about an inch (2.5 cm) apart.
3. Wrap a small piece of masking tape around one end of each piece of yarn to make a "sewing needle." Tie the end of the yarn without tape onto a top hole of the pair of hearts.
4. Give each student a pair of paper hearts with a strand of yarn.
5. Show students how to sew the hearts together using the yarn.
6. Ask students to decorate their heart envelopes with stickers.
7. Help children use the liquid embroidery paint or glitter glue to write their names on the front of the heart envelopes.
8. Have students place their Valentine's Day cards into their heart envelopes.

Activity Cards #3 and #4

Activity Card #3: Heart Fishing

Supplies:

- 2- or 3-inch (5- or 8-cm) horseshoe magnets
- two yard sticks or meter sticks
- string
- scissors
- construction paper, various colors
- Heart-Shaped Fish (page 165)
- large paper clips
- blue butcher paper
- Valentine stickers (optional)

Instructions:

1. Make two fishing poles. For each fishing pole, tie a piece of string onto one end of a yard stick or meter stick (fishing pole). Cut the string (fishing line) so that it is about the same length as the "pole." Tie the loose end of the string to a horseshoe magnet (fish hook).

2. Make several sets of heart-shaped fish in a variety of colors. Pick a skill that you would like to reinforce with this activity. You may wish to write math problems, reading vocabulary words, color words, letters of the alphabet, etc., on each fish.

3. Attach a large paper clip to the mouth of each fish.

4. Cut the blue butcher paper in the shape of a pond. Place the butcher paper on the floor. Then put the fish face-up on the butcher paper.

5. Have two students go fishing at a time. Once a fish is caught, have the student complete the task (e.g. add, subtract, read a vocabulary or color word, identify a letter).

6. You may wish to give students Valentine stickers for participation, trying their best, and showing good sportsmanship.

Extension: Make available several Valentine books for students to enjoy.

Activity Card #4: Valentine Heart Pillows

Supplies:

- white fabric
- chalk
- Heart Pillow Pattern (page 166)
- scissors
- fabric crayons
- an iron
- pillow stuffing material
- sewing machine
- pink, red, or purple thread

Instructions:

1. You may wish to enlist the help of a parent volunteer for sewing the pillows.

2. Make two fabric hearts per student. For each fabric heart, trace around the heart pattern, using a piece of chalk. Then cut out the fabric heart.

3. Give each student two fabric hearts. Ask youngsters to use fabric crayons to color pictures on their fabric hearts.

4. Iron the fabric hearts according to the directions on the fabric crayon boxes.

5. Sew the hearts together leaving a space open for students to insert the stuffing. Help students stuff their pillows. Then finish sewing the pillows.

Activity Card #5

Activity Card #5: My Love Booklet

Supplies:

- medium-sized white board or chalkboard
- My Love Booklet, one per student (page 167)
- scissors
- pencils
- crayons, markers, or colored pencils
- stapler and staples

Instructions:

1. Draw a giant heart on the white board or chalkboard.

2. Encourage students to brainstorm a list of things they love. Write students' ideas in the giant heart you have drawn on the board.

3. Distribute the copies of My Love Booklet to students.

4. Have students fill in the blanks on their My Love Booklet activity sheet. Depending on your students' skill level, you may wish to have students dictate the things they love while you write their ideas in the blanks.

5. Remind youngsters that they can refer to the list on the board.

6. Invite children to use crayons, markers, or colored pencils to draw pictures to go with the words they have written in each blank.

7. Have students cut apart the booklet pages. Provide assistance as needed.

8. Help students put the pages in order.

9. Staple the booklets together along the left-hand side.

10. Have students write their names on the front cover of their booklets.

11. Invite students to share their booklets with the group.

Extension: Encourage students to write and illustrate their own Valentine's Day poems.

Award Certificate

Give students the Valentine's Special Day Award Certificate after they have completed all five center activities. You may prefer to fill in individual student names ahead of time.

✂ -

Congratulations to _____

for completing the

Valentine's Special Day Centers!

Happy Valentine's Day

_____
Teacher

_____
Date

✂ -

Congratulations to _____

for completing the

Valentine's Special Day Centers!

Happy Valentine's Day

_____
Teacher

_____
Date

Heart Animals

Cat

Dog

Fish

Butterfly

Teddy Bear

Bunny

Heart Patterns

Heart-Shaped Fish

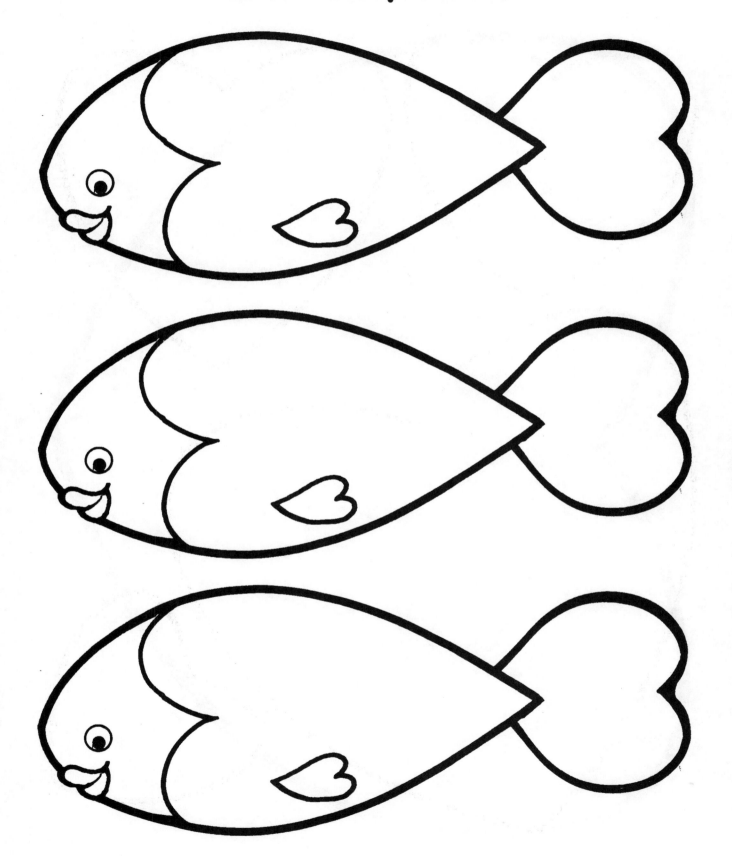

Heart Pillow Pattern

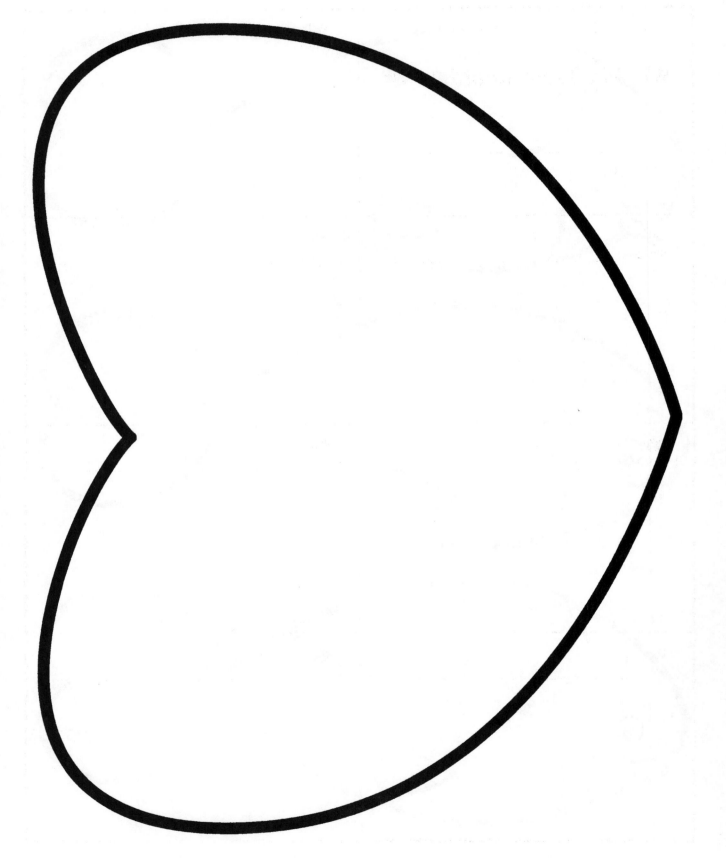

My Love Booklet

❤ **My Love Booklet** ❤

By _____

❤ I love _____ .

1

❤ I love _____ .

2

❤ I love _____ .

3

❤ I love _____ .

4

❤ I love _____ .

5

❤ I love _____ .

6

❤ I love _____ .

7

Snack Ideas and Recommended Book

After students complete the five centers, invite them to enjoy one of the following snacks.

WARNING: Be sure to ask parents if their children have any food allergies or dietary restrictions.

Supplies:

- heart-shaped sugar cookies, one per student
- canned pink frosting
- plastic knives, one per student
- candy hearts

- sprinkles
- paper plates, one per student
- milk
- paper or plastic cups, one per student

Instructions:

Sugar cookies are a favorite snack for the Valentine's Special Day. Give each child a heart-shaped sugar cookie and some frosting, candy hearts, and sprinkles on a paper plate, as well as a plastic knife. Show children how to carefully use the knife to spread the frosting on the cookie. Allow students to spread frosting on their cookies. Then encourage youngsters to decorate their cookies with the candy hearts and sprinkles. Serve each student a cup of milk.

Supplies:

- cake mix
- cake mix ingredients and cooking tools, as listed on the package
- one round and one square-shaped baking pan (**Note:** The diameter of the round pan should be the same as the length of one side of the square pan.)
- large plate

- canned pink frosting
- knife (for adult use only)
- candy hearts
- paper plates, one per student
- milk
- paper or plastic cups, one per student

Instructions:

Another snack idea is to make a giant heart-shaped cake. To do this, prepare the cake mix according to the directions on the back of the package. Pour the batter into the round and square pans. Bake the cake. Then allow it to cool thoroughly. Place the square cake on the large plate. Cut the round cake in half. Place the flat side of the round cake halves on adjacent sides of the square cake.

Cover the cake with frosting and decorate it with candy hearts. Give each student a piece of cake on a paper plate and a cup of milk.

Recommended Book: On Valentine's Special Day, read aloud *Clifford's First Valentine's Day* written by Norman Bridwell (Scholastic, 1996). If students are older, *The Berenstain Bears' Comic Valentine* by Stan and Jan Berenstain (Scholastic, 1997) may be more appropriate.

Presidents' Birthdays
Whole Class Activity

Supplies:

- *A Picture Book of George Washington* (Holiday House, 1995) and *A Picture Book of Abraham Lincoln* (Holiday House, 1990) by David A. Adler
- President for a Day, one per student (page 170)
- white construction paper, one piece per student
- crayons, colored pencils, or markers
- two plastic or Styrofoam bowls
- stapler and staples
- white butcher paper
- pencils
- red and blue water-based paints
- paintbrushes
- large table

Instructions:

Ahead of time, use a pencil to draw an American flag on a piece of white butcher paper that will fit onto your bulletin board. Place the flag on a large table or two tables pushed together.

Discuss the birthdays of George Washington and Abraham Lincoln. Then read aloud the storybooks *A Picture Book of George Washington* and *A Picture Book of Abraham Lincoln*. Lead a discussion about these famous presidents.

Distribute the President for a Day activity sheet. On the chalkboard, draw a three-column chart with the headings *Home, School,* and *Classroom.* Ask students to pretend they have been selected to be president for a day. Tell them to brainstorm ideas about the kinds of new rules they would make if they were president. They should include rules for home, school, and the classroom. Record students' suggestions under the appropriate headings of the chart on the chalkboard. Depending on the skill level of your students, have youngsters fill out their own activity sheets or allow children to dictate their ideas for you to record on their activity sheets. Remind students that they may refer to the list on the chalkboard when completing the activity sheet.

Give each student a piece of white construction paper. On the chalkboard, write the title *My Presidential Self-Portrait.* Ask students to copy the title at the top of the construction paper. Explain what a self-portrait is. Encourage students to draw a picture of themselves as presidents. You may wish to invite students to draw their presidential pets as well.

Make available paintbrushes and bowls of red and blue water-based paints. While the class is drawing their self-portraits, invite two or three students at a time to help paint the huge American flag to be used on the bulletin board. When the flag is finished, allow the paint to dry.

Display the American flag that students have painted on a bulletin board. Place the presidential self-portraits and President for a Day activity sheets around the flag. If there is not enough room on the bulletin board for the self-portraits and activity sheets, simply place the self-portraits over children's activity sheets and staple only at the top so the first page can be flipped up to reveal the second page. Invite students to take turns sharing one or two of their favorite rules that they wrote on the President for a Day activity sheet.

President for a Day

Name: _____ Date: _____

If I were president for a day, I would make these new rules for my home, my school, and my classroom.

Rules for my home:

1. _____

2. _____

3. _____

Rules for my school:

1. _____

2. _____

3. _____

Rules for my classroom:

1. _____

2. _____

3. _____

Buddy Time Activities

Feelings Booklets

As part of the Valentine unit, have the big buddies help their little buddies make a Feelings Booklet (pages 172 and 173). Reproduce the booklet pages, one set per student. You may wish to enlist the help of parent volunteers or the big buddies to help you make the booklets. To make each booklet, follow these directions: Cut the set of pages in half. Place the pages in order. Fold a piece of construction paper in half. Place the booklet pages inside the folded piece of construction paper. Staple along the fold of the construction paper. This will be the top of the booklet. On the front cover, write the title *Feelings Booklet*.

To prepare students for this activity, read some books about feelings during the regularly scheduled buddy time. Two suggestions are *Feelings* by Aliki Brandenberg (William Morrow and Company, 1986) and *Sometimes I Feel Like a Mouse* by Jeanne Modesitt (Scholastic, 1996). After sharing these books, have the big buddies help their little buddies fill out their booklets. The buddies can work together to illustrate the pages. Have little buddies write their names on the front cover. Save these booklets. Then, at parent-teacher conferences, you may wish to ask students to share their booklets with their parents. Sometimes these booklets are very insightful about a student's true feelings.

Friendship Cake

Draw a large picture of a heart and a chef hat on the white board or chalkboard. Reproduce the Friendship Cake Recipe activity sheet (page 174), making one for each pair of buddies.

Ask big and little buddies to brainstorm a list of friendly words. Write their suggestions in the heart you have drawn on the board. Then have big and little buddies brainstorm a list of cooking words. Write their suggestions in the chef's hat you have drawn on the board. You may wish to provide a few examples of each kind of word. See the suggestions below.

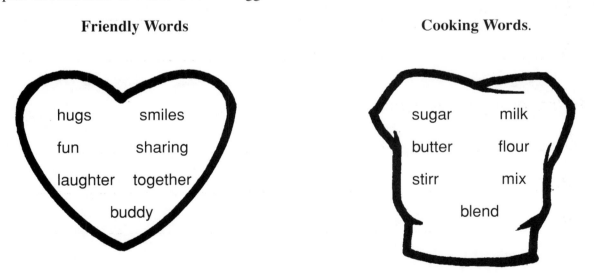

Distribute the Friendship Cake Recipe activity sheet to the buddies. Remind youngsters that they may use the lists you have written on the board to help them fill in the blanks on the activity sheet.

Allow time for students to share their recipes. Then collect all of the activity sheets and place them in a class cookbook

Feelings Booklet

I feel HAPPY when _____

_____ .

1

I feel ANGRY when _____

_____ .

2

Feelings Booklets *(cont.)*

I feel SAD when _____

_____ .

3

I feel SCARED when _____

_____ .

4

Friendship Cake Recipe

Date: _____

Big Buddy's Name: _____

Little Buddy's Name: _____

Ingredients:

_____ cups of _____

_____ cups of _____

_____ teaspoons of _____

_____ tablespoons of _____

secret ingredient: _____

Instructions:

To make the cake batter, _____.

Bake for _____ hours and _____ minutes at 350 degrees.

Allow the cake to cool. Then spread _____
on top. Share some cake with a friend.

Here's a picture of our friendship cake.

Spider Backpack Buddy

February Theme: Valentine's Day

Backpack Buddy: small stuffed spider (include a small heart-shaped pillow)

Storybook: *How Spider Saved Valentine's Day* by Robert Kraus (Scholastic, 1986)

Supplies:
- journal
- Letter from Spider Backpack Buddy (page 176)
- Journal Assignment, one per student (page 177)
- backpack
- Spider Backpack Buddy

Instructions:

You may wish to make the writing journals from portfolios with fasteners. Be sure there are enough journal pages (copies of page 177) for every student in the classroom to complete the writing assignment. Also place a copy of the Letter from Spider Backpack Buddy inside the journal. The homework assignment is described for parents and students in this letter. However, you may prefer to explain the assignment to students before they take it home.

For this journal assignment, students read the book *How Spider Saved Valentine's Day.* Then children make a special Valentine's Day card, with an original Valentine's Day poem or joke, for the class.

Before sending the backpack home with a different child each day, check to be sure it has the small stuffed spider and heart-shaped pillow, the book *How Spider Saved Valentine's Day,* and the writing journal. Remind the student who is taking these materials home to return the backpack and its contents the next school day. When it is the next school day, allow time for the student who took the backpack home to share his/her journal writing assignment with the class.

Be sure every student has an opportunity to take the backpack home. After all students have completed the writing assignment, make the journal a permanent addition to your classroom library.

Letter from Spider Backpack Buddy

Hello!

Please don't be afraid of me. I'm a very friendly spider who loves February, the month that includes Valentine's Day! You can probably tell that Valentine's Day is my favorite holiday from the heart-shaped pillow I keep with me. You and your parents will read about me in *How Spider Saved Valentine's Day.* When you are done with the story, you will realize how friendly I am and what a big heart I have.

After you read *How Spider Saved Valentine's Day,* use a page in this journal to make a Valentine card for your classmates. On the journal page, write a cute poem or joke on it.

Here's an example of a Valentine poem I wrote.

> *Some don't want me to spend the night,*
> *They fear I'll give them a big fright.*
> *Please don't scream or sound an alarm,*
> *I promise I won't bite your arm.*
> *I'm only here to sleep and say,*
> *Have a super Valentine's Day!*

Be creative and have fun making up your own Valentine poem or joke.

Please remember to put the book *How Spider Saved Valentine's Day,* this journal, and me and my pillow inside the backpack and return all of these things to your teacher. You will get to share your Valentine card with the class, and another student will get to take me home.

Bye for now,

Spider

Journal Assignment

Dear Classmates,

Here is my Valentine poem or joke for you.

_____

_____

_____

_____

_____

_____

_____

_____

_____

_____

_____

_____

Yours truly,

_____

Art & Poetry Activities

Heart-Shaped Cat

Supplies:

- Heart-Shaped Cat Pattern (page 180)
- pink construction paper, one piece per student and one for demonstration
- large white piece of construction paper, one per student
- glue
- markers or crayons
- "The Heart-Shaped Cat" poem and "February" title (top half of page 179)
- Favorite Memories, one per student (page 37)

Instructions:

Reproduce the heart patterns on pink construction paper, making one set per student. Give students the pink construction paper hearts and the large white construction paper. Show students how to cut out the pink hearts, arrange the hearts in the shape of a cat, and glue the heart-shaped cat onto one half of the white construction paper. Have youngsters follow your example. Tell students to use the markers or crayons to add details to the cat's face. Distribute the top half of page 179 to students. Read the poem to the class. Ask students to cut out and then glue the poem "The Heart-Shaped Cat" beside the cat picture. Distribute the Favorite Memories activity sheet, and help students complete it. Then have students glue it onto the back of the white construction paper.

Presidents' Birthdays

Supplies:

- "Two Presidents' Birthdays" poem and "February" title, one per student (bottom half of page 179)
- Star Pattern (page 179)
- sponges, one per student
- scissors
- red and blue paint
- plastic or Styrofoam bowls, two for every pair of students
- white construction paper, one piece per student
- large red or blue piece construction paper, one per student
- Favorite Memories, one per student (page 37)

Instructions:

Use the star pattern to cut sponges into the shape of stars. Give each pair of students some red paint in a bowl and blue paint in a bowl. Distribute the sponges and white construction paper. Tell students to use the sponges to paint red and blue stars at random or in a pattern on the white construction paper. Allow the paint to dry. Give each student a large piece of red or blue construction paper and a copy of the bottom half of page 179. Read aloud the poem "Two Presidents' Birthdays" to the class. Ask students to cut out the poem and the "February" title. Help students mount their artwork, the poem, and the title on a piece of large red or blue construction paper. If students have not already done a Favorite Memories activity sheet, help them complete one now. Tell them to glue it onto the back of the large construction paper.

February Poems

The Heart-Shaped Cat

My heart-shaped cat would like to say,

"Have a Happy Valentine's Day!"

'Cause she can only say, "Meow!"

But my sweet cat does not know how,

Purring is what she likes to do,

And "Purr, purr, purr," means "I love you!"

The Heart-Shaped Cat
Pattern

February

Two Presidents' Birthdays

President Washington —

Gave this country a good start.

President Lincoln —

Freed the slaves to do his part.

So to honor these leaders, we give a cheer

And celebrate their birthdays every year!

Star Pattern

February

Heart-Shaped Cat Pattern

Thematic Pins & Magnets

Valentine's Day is always a fun time to give and receive gifts. Patterns are provided below and on page 182. The teddy bear pin shown below has a special message on it. You can use this message or any other you desire. Alternate messages may include "Hug me!" or "I give hugs!" or "Sam's Bear."

Instructions for the teddy bear pin are given below. Additional directions, as well as other ideas for materials to use when creating these gifts, are provided on page 9 of the How to Use Thematic Teaching Ideas section of this book.

Supplies:

- teddy bear pattern (below)
- white vinyl
- white and black liquid embroidery paint
- pin or magnetic strip, one per pattern
- "I love you!" heart pattern (below)
- red vinyl
- glue

Instructions:

1. Trace the bear pattern onto white vinyl and the "I love you!" heart pattern onto red vinyl. Make one of each pattern per student.

2. Help students cut out their white vinyl bears and red vinyl hearts.

3. Tell students to use the black liquid embroidery paint to add the details (face, ears, hands, feet) to the vinyl bear.

4. Use the white liquid embroidery paint to write a message on each vinyl heart.

5. Allow the liquid embroidery paint to dry.

6. Have students glue the red heart onto the stomach of the bear.

7. Help youngsters glue a pin or magnetic strip onto the back of the bear.

February Patterns

Happy Valentine's Day!

Be Mine!

Valentine's Day Videotaping Ideas

The general directions for how to make a Class Video Book are on page 10 of the How to Use Thematic Teaching Ideas section of this book.

Allow time for students to learn and practice the poem "Love Is Like a Magic Penny" (below). You may wish to have youngsters use hand motions to accompany the action words of the verses. As an alternative, have students sing the words.

Reproduce the Valentine Heart Pattern (page 184) on red construction paper for students. Give each child one paper heart to cut out. Tell students to use a black fine-point marker to write the name of something or someone they love on the heart. Examples include: Mom and Dad, pet names, favorite ice cream flavors.

For this Valentine's segment, begin by saying, *Welcome to the month of February. Students have memorized a special poem entitled "Love Is Like a Magic Penny." It's about giving love away. We hope you enjoy it.*

Videotape students reciting or singing "Love Is Like a Magic Penny."

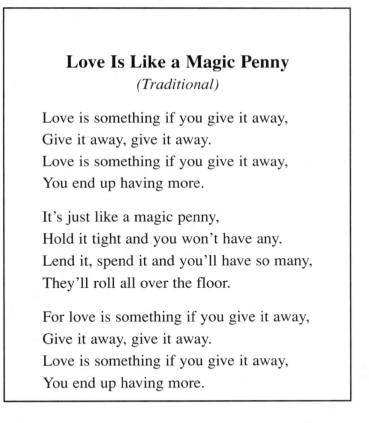

Love Is Like a Magic Penny
(Traditional)

Love is something if you give it away,
Give it away, give it away.
Love is something if you give it away,
You end up having more.

It's just like a magic penny,
Hold it tight and you won't have any.
Lend it, spend it and you'll have so many,
They'll roll all over the floor.

For love is something if you give it away,
Give it away, give it away.
Love is something if you give it away,
You end up having more.

For the final part of this videotaping session, introduce each student. After you introduce a student, have that child hold up his or her paper heart.

At the very end of the Valentine's Day segment, have students smile at the camera, wave, and say all together, *Happy Valentine's Day, Mom and Dad!*

 #3100 Year-Round Units for Early Childhood

Valentine Heart Pattern

March Themes:
Dinosaurs and St. Patrick's Day

Section Contents

Bibliography

Hopkins, T. *1001 Best Web Sites for Educators.* Teacher Created Materials, 2000. URL updates are available at the following address: http://www.teachercreated.com

Dinosaurs

Berenstain, Stan and Jan. *The Berenstain Bears and the Missing Dinosaur Bone.* Beginner Books, 1987.

Berenstain Bears and the Missing Dinosaur Bone. Videotape. Random House Video, 1990. 20 minutes.

Brandenberg, Aliki. *Fossils Tell of Long Ago.* HarperCollins Children's Books, 1990.

The Busasaurus. Videotape. Scholastic Kid Vision, 1997. 30 minutes.

Carrick, Carol. *Patrick's Dinosaurs.* Houghton Mifflin, 1985.

—————. *What Happened to Patrick's Dinosaurs?* Houghton Mifflin, 1989.

Fleischman, Paul. *Time Train.* HarperCollins Children's Books, 1991.

Hiawyn, Oram. *A Boy Wants a Dinosaur.* Farrar Straus Giroux, 1993.

Maynard, Christopher. *The Best Book of Dinosaurs.* Larousse Kingfisher Chambers, 1998.

Most, Bernard. *ABC T-Rex.* Harcourt Brace, 2000.

—————. *If the Dinosaurs Came Back.* Red Wagon, 1995.

St. Patrick's Day

Bateman, Teresa. *Leprechaun Gold.* Holiday House, 1999.

Korman, Justine. *The Luckiest Leprechaun.* Troll Communications, 2000.

Robertson, Ivan T. *Jack and the Leprechaun.* Random House Books for Young Readers, 2000.

Shute, Linda. *Clever Tom and the Leprechaun.* Scholastic, 1990.

Activity Cards #1 and #2

Activity Card #1: Fossil Prints

Supplies:

- nonfiction dinosaur book such as *Fossils Tell of Long Ago* by Aliki Brandenberg (HarperCollins Children's Books, 1990)
- brick red ceramic clay
- kite string
- small paper plates, one per student
- kiln (optional)

1. Ahead of time, use the kite string to cut lumps of clay, one per student. Shape each lump of clay into a tennis-size ball.
2. When students arrive at the center, use a nonfiction children's dinosaur book, such as *Fossils Tell of Long Ago* by Aliki Brandenberg (HarperCollins Children's Books, 1990), to review what a fossil is.
3. Give each student a ball of clay on a small paper plate. Explain to students they will use the clay to make fossil-like handprints.
4. Have students flatten the clay ball and press one hand into it to make a handprint.
5. Place the clay handprints in a safe place while the clay dries.
6. Allow the clay to air-dry for approximately one week. If you prefer, you can fire the clay in a kiln. However, this is not necessary.

Extension: Obtain dinosaur puzzles for students to assemble. A couple of huge rug area dinosaur puzzles are always fun and help students learn the art of cooperation.

Activity Card #2: Dinosaur Strings and P.E. Games

Supplies:

- one piece of green yarn, 90 feet (27 m) in length
- one piece of brown yarn, 30 feet (9 m) in length
- one piece of yellow yarn, 12 feet (3.6 m) in length
- wide masking tape or duct tape
- Dinosaur Patterns (page 191, optional)

Instructions:

1. After you have cut the yarn to the lengths specified above, stretch out the three pieces along the ground so they are parallel and about 3 feet (0.9 m) apart from each other. Use wide masking tape or duct tape to secure the ends of each piece of yarn to the ground.
2. Tell students that the three pieces of yarn represent the lengths of three different dinosaurs. The green yarn represents the length of the brontosaurus, which was renamed the apatosaurus; the brown yarn represents the length of the triceratops; and the yellow yarn represents the length of the pteranodon. You may wish to show pictures of these three dinosaurs using the Dinosaur Patterns provided for Activity Card #4.
3. Ask students to compare and contrast the sizes of these three dinosaurs using the pieces of yarn. Example: The apatosaurus is longer than the triceratops.
4. Have students do different movements as they move up and down the pieces of yarn. For example, students could scissor-walk, tiptoe, run, walk backwards, hop, crawl, etc., the length of each dinosaur.

Activity Cards #3 and #4

Activity Card #3: Dinosaur Dig

Supplies:

- 10–12 small to medium-sized toy plastic dinosaurs
- Dinosaur Dig, one per student (page 190)
- small plastic shovels and rakes
- sandbox or tub filled with sand
- crayons or markers

Instructions:

1. Ahead of time, bury the toy dinosaurs in the sandbox or tub.
2. Explain to students that they are going to pretend to be paleontologists, which are scientists who study dinosaur fossils.
3. Say, *Most paleontologists find dinosaur fossils scattered and buried in layers of earth. These scientists have to put the fossils together like the pieces of a puzzle.*
4. Tell students that today they will dig for whole toy dinosaurs buried in some sand.
5. Have students take turns using shovels and rakes to dig for the toy dinosaurs in the sand box or tub.
6. Distribute the Dinosaur Dig activity sheets to students. Ask children to draw pictures of the dinosaur(s) they find in the sandbox or tub.
7. After students are done with the drawings, ask them to bury the dinosaurs again for the next group.

Activity Card #4: Dinosaur Graph

Supplies:

- Dinosaur Patterns (page 191)
- scissors
- tape
- yarn
- small or medium-sized sticky notes, one per student
- pencils, crayons, or markers

Instructions:

1. On a wall, create the lines of a graph using yarn. Use the Dinosaur Patterns to label the graph.
2. Ask students to decide which dinosaur shown on the graph is their favorite.

	Gabe	Maria			
	Lee	Sharon	Bob	Rita	
	J.P.	Dave			

3. Give each   sticky note. Ask students to write their names on the sticky notes and place   the graph, next to the dinosaurs that are their favorites.
4. Discuss t   n with students. Ask students to read and interpret the data represented by the gr p ample questions: *How many votes did the triceratops get? Which dinosaur had the most votes? Which dinosaur had the least votes? How many votes did the triceratops and stegasaurus get altogether?*

Activity Card #5

Activity Card #5: Dino Pets

Supplies:

- small rocks, sticks, dried leaves, and grass
- small resealable plastic bag
- ceramic clay
- small plastic dinosaurs, one per student plus some extras
- Dino Pets, one label per student (page 192)
- pencils
- shoeboxes with lids, one per student

Instructions:

1. You may wish to ask parents to send empty shoeboxes to school with their children.

2. Give each student a small resealable plastic bag. Take students outside to collect small rocks, sticks, dried leaves, and grass. Remind children not to harm living plants.

3. Return to the classroom, and ask students to pick out a plastic pet dinosaur.

4. Give each student a small amount of clay. Have youngsters make pea-size balls out of the clay. Tell children that the clay balls will represent dinosaur eggs.

5. Distribute the labels from the Dino Pets activity sheet and the shoeboxes to students. Tell youngsters to name their pet dinosaurs. Help students write the names of their pet dinosaurs on the activity sheet label.

6. Ask students to glue the activity sheet label onto one side of the shoebox.

7. Have students use the small rocks, sticks, dried leaves, and grass to make a nest for the pet dinosaur inside the shoebox. Tell them to place their clay dinosaur eggs in the nest. Then have them place the toy dinosaur in the nest.

8. Show children how to use a pencil point to poke holes in the lid of a shoebox. Explain that these are breathing holes so the pet dinosaur has plenty of air.

9. Allow students to poke holes in the lids of their shoeboxes.

10. Invite students to introduce their pet dinosaurs to the group.

11. You may wish to have children tell what they do to care for their pet dinosaurs.

Extension: Obtain dinosaur puzzles for students to assemble. A couple of huge dinosaur puzzles are always fun and help students learn the art of cooperation.

Award Certificate

Give students the Dinosaurs' Special Day Award Certificate after they have completed all five center activities. You may prefer to fill in individual student names ahead of time.

✂ -

Congratulations to _____

for completing the

Dinosaurs' Special Day Centers!

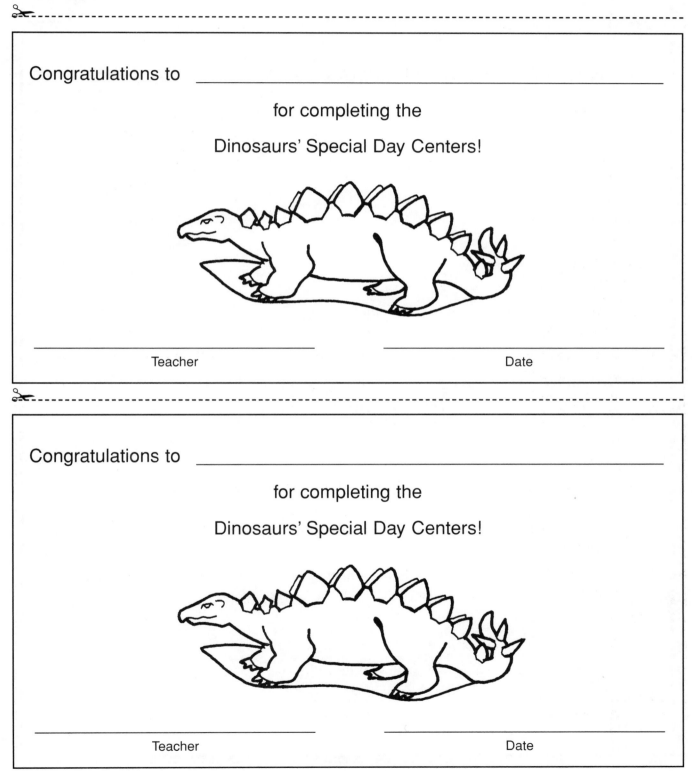

_____   _____
Teacher   Date

✂ -

Congratulations to _____

for completing the

Dinosaurs' Special Day Centers!

_____   _____
Teacher   Date

Dinosaur Dig

Name: _____ Date: _____

This is what the dinosaur(s) I found during the Dinosaur Dig looked like.

Dinosaur Patterns

Pteronodon

Tyrannosaurus Rex

Stegosaurus

Triceratops

Apatosaurus

Ankylosaurus

Dino Pets

Name: _____ Date: _____

My pet dinosaur's name is _____ .

Name: _____ Date: _____

My pet dinosaur's name is _____ .

Name: _____ Date: _____

My pet dinosaur's name is _____ .

Name: _____ Date: _____

My pet dinosaur's name is _____ .

Name: _____ Date: _____

My pet dinosaur's name is _____ .

Name: _____ Date: _____

My pet dinosaur's name is _____ .

Name: _____ Date: _____

My pet dinosaur's name is _____ .

Name: _____ Date: _____

My pet dinosaur's name is _____ .

Snack Ideas and Recommended Book

Supplies:

- plastic berry baskets, one per student
- green cellophane grass (usually available at craft stores)
- candy eggs, chocolate-covered almonds, malt balls
- plastic dinosaurs, one per student (optional)
- graham crackers
- napkins with dinosaur pictures (optional)
- milk
- paper or plastic cups

WARNINGS: Ask parents if their children have any food allergies or dietary restrictions. Please note that young children can choke on nuts.

Instructions:

Ahead of time, ask parents to send plastic berry baskets to school.

Invite youngsters to enjoy a snack of dinosaur eggs nestled sweetly in a bed of green cellophane grass after they have completed all five centers. Use clean berry baskets to make the dinosaur nests. Place green cellophane grass in the baskets. Then place candy eggs, chocolate covered almonds, or malt balls on the cellophane grass.

To add an extra element of realism and fun, you may wish to place a plastic dinosaur in each nest to guard the eggs.

In addition to the nests, serve each student a graham cracker. If available, place the graham crackers on napkins with dinosaur pictures. Give each child a cup of milk to drink.

Recommended Book: On Dinosaurs' Special Day, read aloud *Dazzle the Dinosaur* written by Marcus Pfister (North-South Books, 2000). This story is by the same author who wrote *The Rainbow Fish* series (North-South Books), and it contains a wonderful storyline with a valuable lesson and beautiful illustrations that captivate a young audience.

St. Patrick's Day Whole Class Activity

Supplies:

- Children's Book: *Clever Tom and the Leprechaun* by Linda Shute (Scholastic, 1990)
- Shamrock Patterns (page 195)
- green paper
- Shamrock Directions (page 196)
- Letter from the King of the Leprechauns (page 197)
- Leprechaun's Note (page 198)
- Leprechaun Picture (page 199)
- Congratulations Note (page 200)
- large basket
- a variety of treats such as gold chocolate coins, shamrock-shaped cookies, and St. Patrick's Day stickers

WARNING: Ask parents if their children have any food allergies or dietary restrictions.

Instructions:

Before beginning this activity, reproduce the Shamrock Patterns on green paper. Be sure you have a total of 25 green shamrocks. Cut out the shamrocks. Then write the Shamrock Directions on the green shamrocks. Write only one direction on each shamrock. Depending on the number of students in your class, you may wish to add or subtract some directions in order to have only one shamrock per student. Regardless of the number of students you have, be sure you keep the last two directions since these lead students to the treasure. Number the shamrocks in order according to the steps you want them to follow to be able to find the treasure.

Read aloud the story entitled *Clever Tom and the Leprechaun*. Have the class discuss the book and how the leprechaun in the story outsmarts Tom.

At a time when students are out of the classroom, such as during recess, a special-area class (music, art, or physical education), or lunch break, mess up the classroom by tipping over chairs, drawing on the chalkboard, and placing books, pencils, papers, and crayons on the tables and floor. Hang the Letter from the King of the Leprechauns where students will see it. Place a shamrock with directions written on it on each student's desk. Place the Leprechaun Picture and the Leprechaun's Note on a low branch of a tree outside your classroom. Hide the basket of treats under your desk with the Congratulations Note.

When students return to the classroom, act upset about the mess. Then find the Letter from the King of the Leprechauns and read it aloud. The letter explains that students should follow the directions on the shamrocks, in order according to the numbers on the shamrocks, to find a treasure that was left by the king of the leprechauns.

Help students read the directions on the shamrocks and do the activities described. Be sure students follow the directions in the order of the numbers on the shamrocks. Most of the activities are directed toward the whole class. After students find the treasure basket, read aloud the Congratulations Note. Allow students to share the treasure of chocolate coins, shamrock cookies, and St. Patrick's Day stickers.

Shamrock Patterns

Shamrock Directions

Write each of the following directions on a green shamrock.

1. Count by 10s to 100.

2. Play "I spy something green."

3. Whisper "I love leprechauns," 3 times.

4. Stand up and sit down 3 times.

5. Count backwards from 10 to 0.

6. Line up in order by the numbers on these shamrocks.

7. Have an adult take you outside to the track or playground.

8. Jog once around the track or playground.

9. Hop like Peter Cottontail 3 times.

10. Go down the slide once.

11. Tap your head softly 3 times.

12. Have the adult take you back to the classroom. Then find something in the classroom that is shaped like a square.

13. Turn the classroom lights on and off 2 times.

14. Draw a rainbow on a white board or chalkboard.

15. Draw a pot of gold under the rainbow.

16. Whisper "I believe in leprechauns" 3 times.

17. Clap 10 times.

18. Count to 10 as you march in place like soldiers.

19. Touch your toes 10 times.

20. Sing your favorite song.

21. Find something in the classroom that is shaped like a circle.

22. Dance an Irish jig.

23. Find something in the classroom that is shaped like a rectangle.

24. Have an adult take you outside. Look up in a tree for a leprechaun with a note. Have the adult read the note.

25. Find the treasure and help pass out the goodies.

Letter from the King of the Leprechauns

Dear Boys and Girls,

I've left a special note on each little table,

Pick up just one if you are able.

Read each note, one at a time

I hope you understand this little rhyme.

If you follow the directions well

My leprechaun friends and I can tell.

If you do each step just right

You'll find a treasure that's out of sight.

Remember to do what my shamrocks say

And have a super St. Patrick's Day!

Sincerely,

King of the Leprechauns

Leprechaun's Note

Dear Boys and Girls,

You've found me hiding up in this tree,

So now I must tell you where the treasure will be.

I've hidden a surprise in your classroom—

Not in a closet, not by a broom.

It's hidden right under your teacher's nose—

The place your teacher sits, by your teacher's toes.

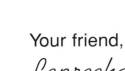  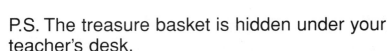

Your friend,

Leprechaun

P.S. The treasure basket is hidden under your teacher's desk.

Leprechaun Picture

Congratulations Note

Congratulations Boys and Girls!

You've followed the directions and knew just what to do.

Hurray, and good for you!

Now, in order to be fair,

The treasure you all must share.

Then it's time for you to have fun,

Playing games outside in the sun!

Just remember as you run and laugh and play

To think about us wee little leprechauns on this wonderful St. Patrick's Day!

Sincerely,

King of the Leprechauns

Buddy Time Activities

Dinosaur Projects

Reproduce the Dinosaur Story form (page 202), making one copy for each pair of buddies. After studying about real dinosaurs, distribute the story form to the buddies. Ask the big buddies to help their little buddies write a dinosaur story using the form. The fictional dinosaur could be named after one of the buddies. (Examples: a dinosaur named Jasonosaurus, a dinosaur named Susieceratops) Allow time for students to share their stories.

For the second dinosaur assignment, reproduce Our Dinosaur Poem (page 203), making one copy for each pair of buddies. To begin, have students brainstorm a list of dinosaurs. Write students' suggestions on a large piece of butcher paper or chart paper. Then have them brainstorm a list of rhyming words. Record these on a separate piece of butcher paper or chart paper. Distribute Our Dinosaur Poem to the buddies. Have the buddies work together to write a dinosaur poem. Encourage youngsters to refer to the lists on butcher or chart paper as they write their poems. Ask both buddies to sign the poem. Allow time for students to share their poems.

Leprechaun Stories

Reproduce the Leprechaun Stories (page 204) and the Leprechaun Puzzle (page 205). Give a half-sheet entitled "Our Leprechaun Story" to each pair of buddies. Ask the big buddies to help their little buddies fill in the blanks to complete the story. Give each pair of buddies a piece of large green construction paper. Have the buddies glue their stories near the bottom of the construction paper. Distribute the Leprechaun Puzzle. Have youngsters color and cut out the puzzle pieces. Then have them put the puzzle together and glue it at the top of the green construction paper. Write *Happy St. Patrick's Day* on the chalkboard. Have students copy this title on the construction paper. You may wish to give students shamrock stickers to place around the Leprechaun Puzzle and the title.

Three Leprechaun Wishes

Reproduce My Three Wishes (page 206) on green paper, making one copy for each pair of buddies.

First read aloud a St. Patrick's Day leprechaun story. One highly recommended book is *Clever Tom and the Leprechaun* by Linda Shute (Scholastic, 1990).

Distribute the My Three Wishes activity sheet to the buddies. Have the little buddies pretend that they have caught a leprechaun who, as a result, has to grant them three wishes. Tell the little buddies to dictate their three wishes to the big buddies. Ask the big buddies to record the wishes on the My Three Wishes activity sheet. Have the big buddies help the little buddies cut out the shamrock.

Invite the little buddies to share their three wishes with the class. Then display the shamrocks in the classroom.

Dinosaur Story

Date: _____

Little Buddy's Name: _____

Big Buddy's Name: _____

My favorite real dinosaur is _____

because _____

_____.

Here is my story about a make-believe dinosaur.

My dinosaur's name is _____.

My dinosaur was born when _____.

It is a boy/girl dinosaur. (Circle one.)

It lives _____.

Its favorite foods are _____.

If my dinosaur could talk, it would say, " _____

_____."

If I could take my dinosaur anywhere, I would take it to _____

_____ .

Here is a question I would like to ask my dinosaur: _____

_____?

When I took my dinosaur for a walk, this is
what happened: _____

_____.

On the back of this paper is a picture of my
make-believe dinosaur.

Our Dinosaur Poem

Date: _____

Little Buddy's Name: _____

Big Buddy's Name: _____

Leprechaun Stories

Our Leprechaun Story

Date: _____

Little Buddy's Name: _____

Big Buddy's Name: _____

My name is _____, and I am a leprechaun. I am
_____ inches tall. I wear _____ and _____ . One
day I played a trick on some children who were looking for my pot of gold.
This is what I did to trick them: _____

_____ .

But the children caught me and took me to _____ .
They were nice to me, and I had fun! The children taught me how to
_____ and _____ . Later, I showed them where I live. I
took them to my house, which is in a _____ .

Our Leprechaun Story

Date: _____

Little Buddy's Name: _____

Big Buddy's Name: _____

My name is _____, and I am a leprechaun. I am
_____ inches tall. I wear _____ and _____ . One
day I played a trick on some children who were looking for my pot of gold.
This is what I did to trick them: _____

_____ .

But the children caught me and took me to _____ .
They were nice to me, and I had fun! The children taught me how to
_____ and _____ . Later, I showed them where I live. I
took them to my house, which is in a _____ .

Leprechaun Puzzle

Color and cut out the leprechaun puzzle. Then put the puzzle together, and glue it onto a piece of green construction paper

My Three Wishes

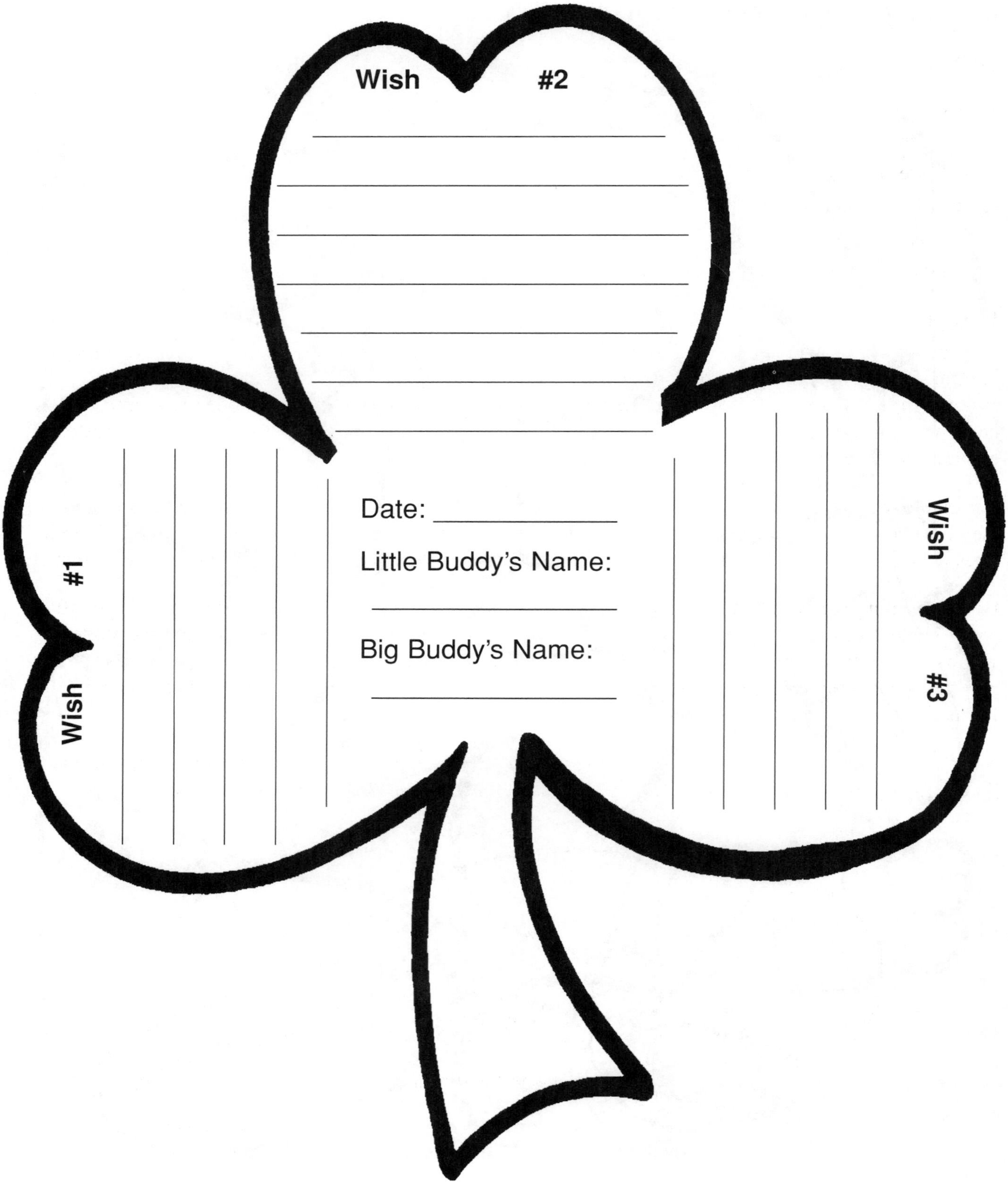

Wish   **#2**

_____

Wish #1

Wish #3

Date: _____

Little Buddy's Name:
_____

Big Buddy's Name:
_____

Dinosaur Backpack Buddy

March Theme: Dinosaurs

Backpack Buddy: small stuffed apatosaurus (brontosaurus)

Storybook: *A Boy Wants a Dinosaur* by Hiawyn Oram and Satoshi Kitamura (Farrar, Straus & Giroux, 1993)

Supplies:
- journal
- Letter from Dinosaur Backpack Buddy (page 208)
- Journal Assignment, one per student (page 209)
- backpack
- Dinosaur Backpack Buddy

Instructions:

You may wish to make the writing journals from portfolios with fasteners. Be sure there are enough journal pages (copies of page 209) for every student in the classroom to complete the writing assignment. Also place a copy of the Letter from Dinosaur Backpack Buddy Inside the journal. The homework assignment is described for parents and students in this letter. However, you may prefer to explain the assignment to students before they take it home.

For this journal assignment, students read the book *A Boy Wants a Dinosaur.* Then students pretend they have a pet baby dinosaur and write to tell what kind it is, what its name is, what it eats, where it likes to play, and so forth. Then students draw a picture of themselves with their pet baby dinosaurs.

Before sending the backpack home with a different child each day, check to be sure it has the small stuffed apatosaurus, the book *A Boy Wants a Dinosaur,* and the writing journal. Remind the student who is taking these materials home to return the backpack and its contents the next school day. When it is the next school day, allow time for the student who took the backpack home to share his/her journal writing assignment with the class.

Be sure every student has an opportunity to take the backpack home. After all students have completed the writing assignment, make the journal a permanent addition to your classroom library.

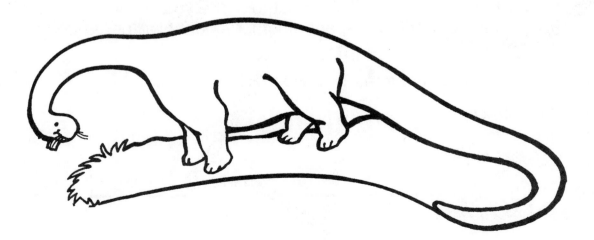

Letter from Dinosaur Backpack Buddy

Waaa! Waaa!

I am very confused! I am a baby dinosaur who recently hatched out of my egg and found myself wandering around your school playground. Your teacher was kind enough to pick me up and put me in this cozy backpack. To make me feel less afraid, your teacher has asked me to get to know you and your classmates. That's why I am getting to spend the night with you.

Going to different children's homes is also helping me learn more about our world. Where are all the giant lizards? I only see little ones — many of which are even smaller than me. Why aren't there any pteranodons flying around in the sky? Our world seems very strange to me, and sometimes I feel scared. Maybe you could help me feel more comfortable by feeding me and playing with me.

You can read about me in the book *A Boy Wants a Dinosaur.* After you read *A Boy Wants a Dinosaur,* please use a page in this journal to write down some things about me, describe some of the things we do together while I am visiting your home, and draw a picture of the two of us.

Please don't forget to put the book *A Boy Wants a Dinosaur,* this journal, and me inside the backpack and return all of these things to your teacher. You will get to share your writing assignment with the class, and another student will get to take me home.

Thanks so much! I already feel better!

Yours truly,

Baby Dinosaur

Journal Assignment

Name: _____ Date: _____

This baby dinosaur is a _____ .

(Tell what type of dinosaur the baby is.)

The baby dinosaur's favorite food is _____ .

I have named the baby dinosaur _____ .

Here are some fun things the baby dinosaur and I did together:

_____

_____

_____

_____

_____

_____

Here is a picture of the baby dinosaur with me.

Art & Poetry Activities

My Pet Dinosaur

Supplies:

- "My Pet Dinosaur" poem and "March" title, one per student (top half of page 211)
- large white construction paper, one piece per student
- scissors
- glue
- Dinosaur Pattern, one per student (page 212)
- green construction paper, one piece per student
- markers or crayons
- full-body photograph of each student (optional)
- Favorite Memories, one per student (page 37)

Instructions:

Distribute the copies of the top half of page 211 and the white construction paper to students. Read aloud the poem. Have students fold the white paper in half so it opens like a book. Have students glue the poem on one half of the construction paper. Reproduce the Dinosaur Pattern on green construction paper. Give each student a green apatosaurus. Tell youngsters to cut out the dinosaur and glue it onto the blank half of the white construction paper. Then have students draw themselves walking the dinosaur with a leash. An optional idea is to have students glue a full-body photograph of themselves onto the construction paper. Then have youngsters draw the dinosaur's leash from their hands in the photograph to the dinosaur's neck. Invite students to add background, such as trees, flowers, butterflies, and the Sun, to their pictures. Distribute the Favorite Memories activity sheet. Help students complete it. Then have students glue it onto the back of the construction paper.

Leprechaun Time

Supplies:

- large piece white construction paper, one per student
- glue
- markers or crayons
- shamrock stickers
- "Leprechaun Time" poem and "March" title, one per student (bottom half of page 211)
- Leprechaun's Sack (page 211)
- Favorite Memories, one per student (page 37)

Instructions:

Distribute the copies of the bottom half of page 211 and the white construction paper to students. Read aloud the poem "Leprechaun Time" to the class. Have students cut out the Leprechaun's Sack, the poem, and the "March" title. Ask students to draw a picture of themselves on one half of the construction paper, and glue the sack so that it looks like they are holding it. Invite students to draw a picture inside the sack of the leprechaun they caught. Have students glue the "Leprechaun Time" poem and "March" title onto the construction paper. Allow students to use some shamrock stickers to add a festive St. Patrick's Day decoration to their pictures. If students have not already done a Favorite Memories activity sheet, help them complete one now. Tell them to glue it onto the back of this artwork.

March Poems

My Pet Dinosaur

If I had a small pet dino,
I couldn't call him my little rhino.
His Indian name would have to be
"One-who-eats-leaves-from-a-tree."
His Irish name might sound silly —
"Long neck, green face, Wee Little Willy."
But in America, land of the free,
"Little Sammy" is who he'll be!
Here I am taking Sammy for a walk —
Pretty soon he just might talk.
And when he does, he'll probably say,
"Scratch my belly, and make my day!"

March

Leprechaun Time

Time to search for treasures of gold

And watch for leprechauns — so I've been told.

Time to wear bright colors of green

And watch for leprechauns, rarely seen.

Time to dance some Irish jigs

And watch for leprechauns in trees or on twigs.

Time to search high and low.

Just watch for leprechauns wherever you go!

March

Dinosaur Pattern

Thematic Pins & Magnets

The dinosaur pin below is one of the easiest and quickest magnets and pins to make. This makes a wonderful gift for students to wear during the dinosaur unit. Other March patterns are included below and on page 214. Allow students to make pins and magnets using any of these pattern selections.

Instructions for the dinosaur pin or magnet are given below. Additional directions, as well as other ideas for materials to use when creating these gifts, are provided on page 9 of the How to Use Thematic Teaching Ideas section of this book.

Supplies:

- apatosaurus pattern (below)
- black and gold liquid fabric paint
- pin or magnetic strip, one per pattern
- light green vinyl
- small plastic eyes, one per pattern
- glue

Instructions:

1. Have students trace the apatosaurus pattern on the light green vinyl.
2. Tell students to cut out the green vinyl dinosaur. Provide assistance as needed.
3. Have students use the black fabric paint to add details such as the mouth, nostrils, and nose.
4. Tell students to use the gold liquid paint to put dots on the apatosaurus's back.
5. Help youngsters glue a plastic eye onto the apatosaurus's face.
6. Help students glue a pin or magnetic strip onto the back of the apatosaurus.

March Patterns

Dinosaur Videotaping Ideas

The general directions for how to make a Class Video Book are on page 10 of the How to Use Thematic Teaching Ideas section of this book.

The four dinosaurs featured in this segment are the stegosaurus, pterodactyl, triceratops, and tyrannosaurus rex. Ahead of time, have students make four dinosaur paper bag puppets, using the patterns on pages 216–219. To make each puppet, tell students to turn the paper bag upside down without opening it. Show them how to glue the puppet's head onto the bottom of the bag. Then show them how to glue the puppet's body under the head. Teach students how to open and close the puppet's mouth as they recite the appropriate part of the poem.

Allow time for students to learn and practice the dinosaur poem (below).

Dinosaurs

I'm a stegosaurus with bony plates upon my back.

I have four sharp tail spikes in case of a T-Rex attack!

I'm a pterodactyl, nesting in the high, high trees.

I like to dive for my tasty meals in the prehistoric seas.

My name is triceratops. I have three horns on my face.

I like to live upon the plains and roam from place to place.

I'm the dreaded T-Rex with teeth six inches long.

I chase and eat other dinosaurs that might not be as strong.

Introduce the dinosaur videotaping segment with a dinosaur puppet. Use this puppet to explain that throughout the month of March, students have been studying about dinosaurs. Have the puppet share that some of these dinosaurs are its long lost relatives and friends.

Videotape students reciting the dinosaur poem while using the four dinosaur puppets. If you prefer, you can divide the class into four groups. Ask each group to hold up a different puppet. As the class recites the poem, have the different groups hold up the appropriate puppets as each type of dinosaur is being described.

At the end of the videotaping session, ask each student to tell which type of dinosaur they like best. Then have students hold up a dinosaur puppet, wave at the camera, and say all together, *Happy dinosaur hunting, Mom and Dad!*

Stegosaurus

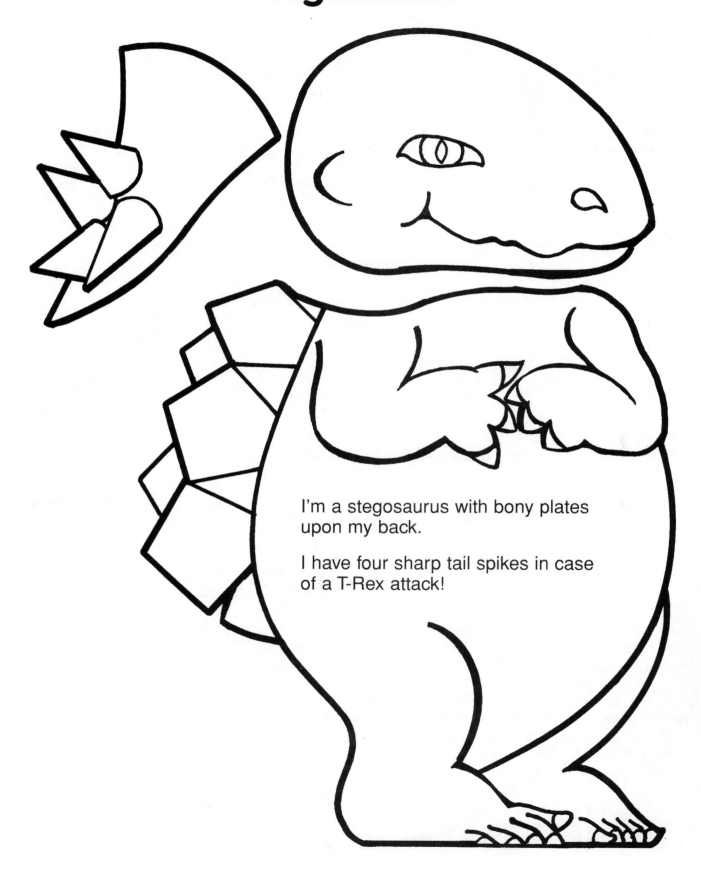

I'm a stegosaurus with bony plates upon my back.

I have four sharp tail spikes in case of a T-Rex attack!

Pterodactyl

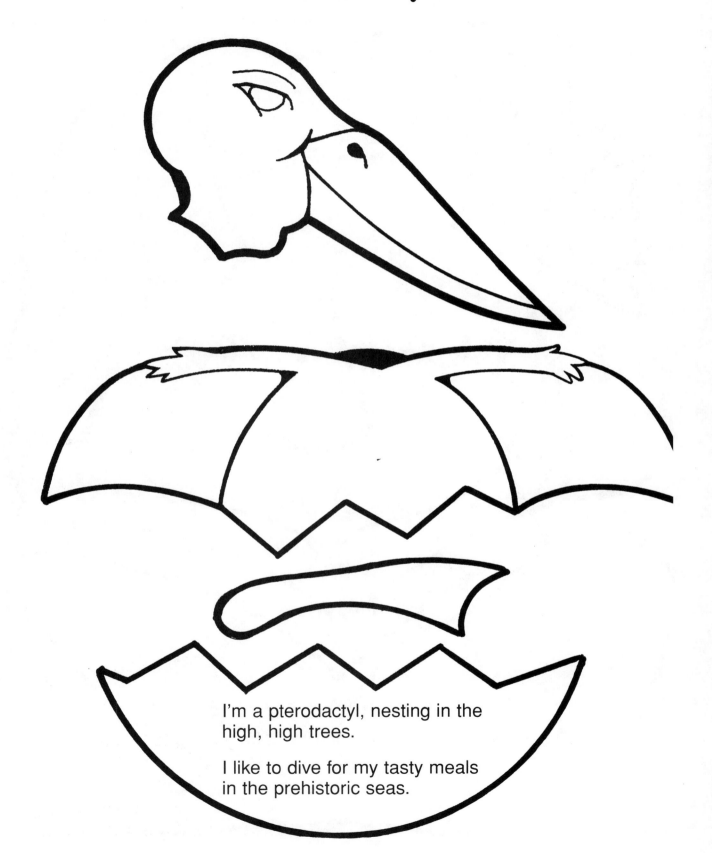

I'm a pterodactyl, nesting in the high, high trees.

I like to dive for my tasty meals in the prehistoric seas.

Triceratops

My name is triceratops. I have three horns on my face.

I like to live upon the plains and roam from place to place.

Tyrannosaurus Rex

I'm the dreaded T-Rex with teeth six inches long.

I chase and eat other dinosaurs that might not be as strong.

April Themes:
Eggs and Easter

Section Contents

Bibliography

Hopkins, T. *1001 Best Web Sites for Educators*. Teacher Created Materials, 2000. URL updates are available at the following address: http://www.teachercreated.com

Eggs

Heller, Ruth. *Chickens Aren't the Only Ones*. Putnam Books for Young Readers, 1999. http://www.aeb.org/ This is the incredible edible egg Web site. It contains egg recipes, egg facts, egg nutritional information, etc.

Easter

Bailey, Carolyn Sherwin. *The Little Rabbit Who Wanted Red Wings*. Putnam, 1988.

Bridwell, Norman. *Clifford's Happy Easter*. Scholastic, 1994.

Brown, Margaret Wise. *The Runaway Bunny*. HarperCollins Children's Books, 1991.

Kroll, Steven. *The Big Bunny and the Easter Egg*. Scholastic, 1988.

Show Me a Story: Based on the Tales of Beatrix Potter (Vol. 1 and 2). Videotape. Family Home Entertainment, 1993. 45 minutes each volume.

The Velveteen Rabbit. Videotape. Random House Video, 1985. 30 minutes.

Williams, Margery. *The Velveteen Rabbit*. Alfred A. Knopf, 1990.

Activity Cards #1 and #2

Activity Card #1: Inside My Egg

Supplies:

- *Chickens Aren't the Only Ones* by Ruth Heller (Penguin Putnam Books for Young Readers, 1999)
- Inside My Egg, one of each page per student (pages 225 and 226)
- scissors
- crayons
- markers
- stapler and staples

Instructions:

1. Read aloud *Chickens Aren't the Only Ones* by Ruth Heller.
2. Have students list the real animals shown in the story *Chickens Aren't the Only Ones* that hatch from eggs. Use the pictures in the book to prompt students. Record the list on the chalkboard.
3. Distribute the Inside My Egg activity sheets to students.
4. Tell students to color the egg on page 225.
5. Ask students to choose an animal from the book. Have them draw a picture of that animal inside the egg on page 226.
6. Have youngsters cut out both eggs.
7. Staple the egg from page 225 on top of the egg from page 226 for students. Point out that the animal inside the egg is hidden.
8. You may wish to have students play a game in which they try to guess what type of animal is hiding inside each egg.

Extension: Collect a variety of books about springtime, Easter, and eggs for students to enjoy.

Activity Card #2: Egg Recipes

Supplies

- white butcher paper, one piece per group
- My Special "Egg Recipe," one per student (page 227)
- crayons
- markers

Instructions:

1. Cut out a large egg shape for each group from white butcher paper.
2. Lead a discussion about how eggs can be prepared (scrambled, deviled, poached, fried, hard-boiled, etc.).
3. Invite students to brainstorm ideas that involve cooking with eggs. Write their suggestions on the large paper egg.
4. Distribute the copies of My Special "Egg Recipe" to students. Ask youngsters to write and illustrate their own egg recipes. Allow younger students to dictate their recipes.
5. Save the egg-shaped recipe cards to make a class recipe book.
6. Encourage students to take the book home to share with their families.

Activity Card #3

Activity Card #3: Plastic Egg Treasure Hunt

Supplies:

- 15 medium-sized plastic eggs
- black permanent marker
- Plastic Egg Directions (page 228)
- colored copier paper
- scissor
- large basket
- candy eggs
- Easter stickers (optional)
- small basket

WARNING: Be sure to ask parents if their children have any food allergies or dietary restrictions.

Instructions:

1. Use the permanent marker to number the outside of the plastic eggs from 1 to 15. **Note:** The number of eggs and directions may be reduced if desired.
2. Reproduce the Plastic Egg Directions on a piece of colored copier paper.
3. Cut apart the directions, and place them inside the plastic eggs. Be sure the number on the directions matches the number on the outside of the egg.
4. While students are not around, hide the fifteen eggs, preferably outside the classroom.
5. Show students the large basket and tell them that they are going to hunt for fifteen plastic eggs. Read the following poem to students.

> *Every egg has a note for all to enjoy.*
> *Do what it says. Be a good girl or boy.*
> *A special treasure you will find.*
> *Divide it equally with each friend.*
> *Then this treasure hunt will come to an end!*

6. Discuss safety rules before allowing students to look for the eggs.
7. Ask students to put the eggs in the basket.
8. After all fifteen eggs have been found, invite youngsters to put the eggs in order from 1 to 15.
9. Have students take turns opening the eggs in order by the numbers written on the eggs.
10. Have youngsters read directions to the group. Encourage all members of the group to follow the directions.
11. After students find the treasure, divide it equally among the members in the group.

Extension: After a group participates in the above activity, you may wish to have the group members put the clues back inside the eggs. Then those students can help hide the eggs for the next group.

Activity Cards #4 and #5

Activity Card #4: Rock Egg Art

Supplies:

- oval-shaped, smooth, medium-sized rocks or paper plates cut into ovals, one per student and one for demonstration
- 5–6 bright colors of water-based paint
- 5–6 plastic or Styrofoam bowls
- small to medium-sized paintbrushes
- one black permanent marker

Instructions:

1. Collect oval-shaped, smooth, medium-sized rocks, or cut paper plates into oval shapes. Give a rock or oval-shaped piece of a paper plate to each student. Point out that the rock or oval-shaped piece of paper plate looks like an egg.

2. Use one egg to show students what to do. Pick one side to be the top of the egg. Demonstrate how to paint the egg using a variety of colors and making different designs, such as stripes, polka dots, and wavy lines, on it.

3. Have students decide which is the top of their eggs. Then tell them to use the permanent marker to write their names on the bottom of their eggs.

4. Allow students to paint the top of their eggs. Allow the paint to dry.

Extension: Cut scratch paper into oval shapes. Allow students to use the ovals to design and color their own paper eggs.

Activity Card #5: Egg Races

Supplies:

- five or six large wooden spoons
- two dozen or more hard-boiled eggs
- plastic tape or wide masking tape
- five or six large handkerchiefs
- colorful egg stickers or nametag labels

WARNING: Be sure you have plenty of space for students to do these races.

Instructions:

1. Egg stickers can be made by coloring ovals on blank nametag labels.

2. Use plastic or wide masking tape to mark the start and finish lines for the races.

3. Discuss safety rules with students before allowing them to compete in the following races.

   Race #1 — Have students line up at the starting line with an egg on a large wooden spoon. Ask them to walk as fast as they can to the finish line, without dropping the egg.

   Race #2 — Have pairs of students place an egg in a handkerchief "hammock." Have the pairs of students race each other by walking sideways to the finish line.

   Race #3 — Have students hold an egg under their chins. Tell them to race to the finish line, without dropping their eggs. Students can be required to walk or run for this race.

   Race #4 — Have students using their wooden spoons as sticks to help roll and push their eggs from the start to the finish lines.

Award Certificate

Give students the Eggs' Special Day Award Certificate after they have completed all five center activities. You may prefer to fill in individual student names ahead of time.

✂ -

Congratulations to _____

for completing the

Eggs' Special Day Centers!

_____   _____
Teacher   Date

✂ -

Congratulations to _____

for completing the

Eggs' Special Day Centers!

_____   _____
Teacher   Date

Inside My Egg

Inside My Egg *(cont.)*

The animal inside my egg is a _____.

Name: _____

Date: _____

My Special "Egg Recipe"

Name: _____ Date: _____

Ingredients:

_____

_____

_____

Instructions:

_____

_____

_____

_____

Plastic Egg Directions

1. Hop like a bunny 5 times.

2. Roll like eggs across the floor.

3. Name 5 animals that hatch from eggs.

4. Count from 1 to 10.

5. Whisper "I love eggs" 3 times.

6. Tell your favorite way to eat eggs.

7. Stand up and touch your toes 10 times.

8. Skip in a circle 2 times.

9. Say something nice about someone.

10. Bend from the waist and touch your toes 10 times.

11. Clap 10 times.

12. Make a funny face.

13. Snap or click your fingers 10 times.

14. Look for a basket with candy eggs.

15. Divide the eggs equally among the members of your group.
    Then eat the eggs.

Snack Ideas and Recommended Book

Supplies:

- egg snacks, such as hard-boiled eggs and miniature egg salad sandwiches, one of each per student
- small paper plates, one per student
- milk (optional)
- plastic or paper cups, one per student (optional)
- yellow construction paper, one piece per student
- paper napkins, one per student
- scissors
- crayons or markers

WARNING: Be sure to ask parents if their children have any food allergies or dietary restrictions.

Instructions:

Ahead of time, prepare egg snacks, such as hard-boiled eggs and mini egg salad sandwiches, for students.

Cut the yellow construction paper and paper napkins into egg shapes. See the sample napkin shown below.

Sample Egg-Shaped Napkin

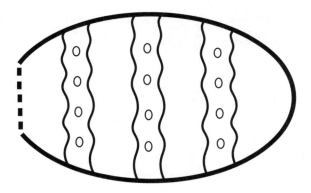

Give each student the egg snacks on a paper plate. You may wish to serve cups of milk. Tell students to use the egg-shaped yellow construction paper as placemats. While youngsters eat their egg snacks, allow them to draw on the placemats.

For entertainment, ask students, one at a time, to share the eggs they made for Inside My Egg (Activity Card #1, page 221). Tell children to give clues to describe the animals they have drawn inside the eggs. Ask the other students to raise their hands and guess what the animals are. Also, you may wish to invite volunteers to read aloud My Special "Egg Recipe" (Activity Card #2, page 221).

Recommended Book: On Eggs' Special Day, read aloud *Chickens Aren't the Only Ones* written by Ruth Heller (Penguin Putnam Books for Young Readers, 1999). This educational book about real animals that hatch from eggs is written in prose and is beautifully illustrated.

Easter Whole Class Activity

Supplies:

- stickers, jelly beans, small foil-wrapped chocolate eggs, and small toys
- plastic eggs, three per student
- black permanent marker
- *Clifford's Easter* by Norman Bridwell (Scholastic, 1994)
- white or brown lunch bags, one per student
- Bunny Bag Basket Pattern, one per student (page 231)
- glue
- scissor
- stapler and staples
- tagboard strips for baskets, one per student
- cellophane grass
- cookies (optional)
- candy
- paper plates, one per student (optional)
- milk (optional)
- plastic or paper cups, one per student (optional)

WARNING: Ask parents if their children have any food allergies or dietary restrictions.

Instructions:

Ahead of time, place treats inside the plastic eggs. Use a permanent marker to write each student's name on three of the eggs. Hide the eggs, preferably outside. If you prefer an indoor location, the eggs may be hidden in your classroom.

Read aloud to the class *Clifford's Easter* and discuss it with students. You may wish to ask students to tell which illustration in the book they like best.

Tell students that because it is to the Easter season, they are going on an Easter egg hunt similar to the one in the story. Give each student a white or brown lunch bag and a copy of the Bunny Bag Basket Pattern. Have youngsters glue the bunny pattern on one side of the bag. Help children cut out the space between the bunny's ears. Staple the top of the bag together, and staple a strip of tagboard to the ears to use as a handle. Give each student some green cellophane grass to place inside the paper bag basket.

Take students to the location where the eggs are hidden. Tell children that the Easter Bunny has hidden three plastic eggs for each of them. Point out that their names will be on the eggs. Allow students to look for the eggs that have their names written on the shells.

After all the eggs are found, tell students to bring their bunny bags back to their tables or desks. Allow youngsters to eat the candies.

You may wish to serve cookies with milk so that students can take their candies home.

Bunny Bag Basket Pattern

Add a tagboard handle.

(Top of Bag)

Cut Out

(Bottom of Bag)

Buddy Time Activities

The Egg

Read aloud the book *Chickens Aren't the Only Ones* by Ruth Heller (Penguin Putnam Books for Young Readers, 1999) to the buddies. Ask students to brainstorm a list of real animals that hatch from eggs. Record their ideas on a large wipe board or chalkboard.

Reproduce the Egg Patterns (page 233) and In Our Egg (page 234). Each pair of buddies gets one egg pattern and a copy of In Our Egg. First have students color and cut out the egg pattern. Tell them to glue the egg pattern onto the In Our Egg activity sheet. Ask the buddies to draw a real animal hatching out of the egg. Then have youngsters fill in the blank at the bottom of the In Our Egg activity sheet. After the buddies have completed the activity, collect the pages to create a class book.

Easter Card

The Easter Card (page 235) is a follow-up to the In Our Egg activity described above. For the front of the card, have the buddies work together to draw a real animal hatching from the egg. Have the little buddies dictate a special Easter or spring message for their big buddies to write inside the card. Invite the buddies to use markers or crayons to make the card more colorful. Encourage the little buddies to take their cards home to their families. As an alternative, you may wish to allow both the big and little buddies to make cards for their families.

Bunny Booklet

Prepare a My Buddy, the Big Bunny, and Me booklet (pages 236–238) for each student by reproducing the pages and stapling each set together. Give the booklets to the buddies. Have youngsters fill in their names on the cover of the booklet. Have each buddy draw himself/herself next to the big bunny on the cover. Have the buddies read the story together. Then have the little buddies dictate a hiding place for the big buddies to fill in the blank on the last page. Allow the buddies to work together to draw a picture of the hidden egg on the last page. When the booklet is completed, encourage the buddies to read the story together several times for extra practice. Then invite the little buddies to take the booklets home to read to their families.

Egg Patterns

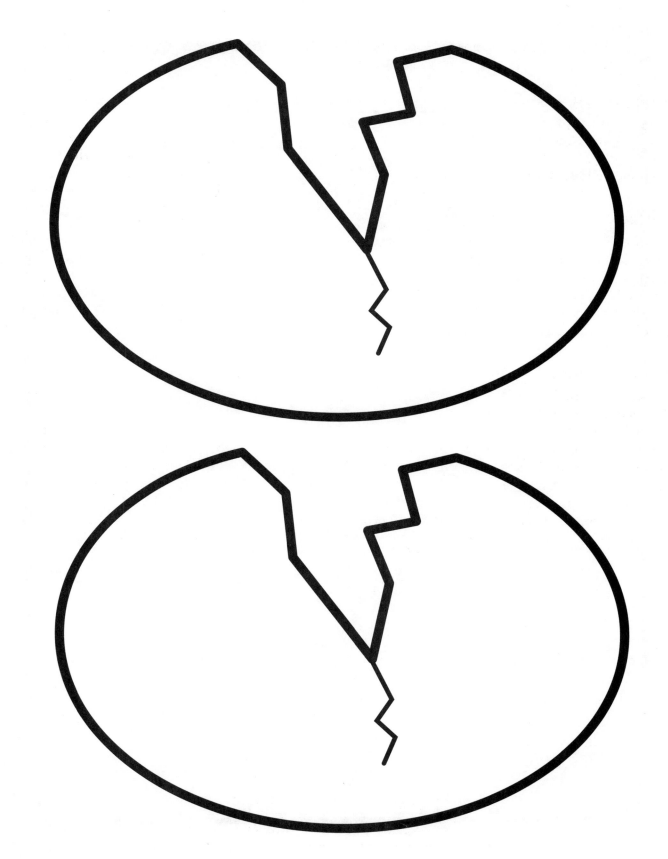

In Our Egg

Date:_____

Little Buddy's Name: _____

Big Buddy's Name: _____

In our egg, there is a _____ .

Easter Card

Fold.

"Hoppy" Easter!

"Look what came out of my egg!"

My Buddy, the Big Bunny, and Me

Date: _____

Little Buddy's Name: _____

Big Buddy's Name: _____

My Buddy, the Big Bunny, and Me *(cont.)*

My buddy, the big bunny, and I hid an egg up a tree.

My buddy, the big bunny, and I hid an egg in the sea.

My buddy, the big bunny, and I hid an egg beside a bee.

My buddy, the big bunny, and I hid an egg under a key.

My buddy, the big bunny, and I hid an egg under my knee.

My Buddy, the Big Bunny, and Me *(cont.)*

_____

This is where my buddy and I hid an egg from the big bunny.

_____

Rabbit Backpack Buddy

April Theme: Easter

Backpack Buddy: small brown stuffed rabbit

Storybook: *The Velveteen Rabbit* written by Margery Williams and illustrated by David Jorgenson (Alfred A. Knopf, 1990)

Supplies:
- journal
- Letter from Rabbit Backpack Buddy (page 240)
- Journal Assignment, one per student (page 241)
- backpack
- Rabbit Backpack Buddy

Instructions:

You may wish to make the writing journals from portfolios with fasteners. Be sure there are enough journal pages (copies of page 241) for every student in the classroom to complete the writing assignment. Also place a copy of the Letter from Rabbit Backpack Buddy inside the journal. The homework assignment is described for parents and students in this letter. However, you may prefer to explain the assignment to students before they take it home.

For this journal assignment, students read the book *The Velveteen Rabbit*. Then they tell about a special stuffed animal or toy that they own. Students pretend that the special stuffed animal or toy comes to life just like the velveteen rabbit does in the story. Students write about some of the things they do with the stuffed animal or toy. Then they draw a picture of this stuffed animal or toy.

Before sending the backpack home with a different child each day, check to be sure it has the small brown stuffed rabbit, the book *The Velveteen Rabbit,* and the writing journal. Remind the student who is taking these materials home to return the backpack and its contents the next school day. When it is the next school day, allow time for the student who took the backpack home to share his/her journal writing assignment with the class.

Be sure every student has an opportunity to take the backpack home. After all students have completed the writing assignment, make the journal a permanent addition to your classroom library.

Letter from Rabbit Backpack Buddy

Hello!

I'm the little rabbit from the special storybook *The Velveteen Rabbit*. You will find a copy of the book in my backpack. In this story, I am finally granted the gift of real life. To find out why this happens, you will need to read the story with your parents.

After you have read *The Velveteen Rabbit,* I want you to think of a special stuffed animal or toy that you own now or that you used to own. Pick a stuffed animal or toy that you love very much. If you can't think of a special stuffed animal or toy, you can use me for this activity. Please use a page in this journal to tell about and draw a picture of your stuffed animal or toy.

Thank you for letting me spend the night with you. I hope you enjoy my story. On your next school day, put the book *The Velveteen Rabbit,* this journal, and me inside the backpack and return everything to your teacher. You will get to share your writing assignment with the class, and another student will get to take me home.

Bye for now!

The Velveteen Rabbit

Journal Assignment

Name: _____ Date: _____

The name of my special stuffed animal or toy is _____ .

I've had this toy since I was _____ years old. It was given to me

by _____ .

One day my special friend came alive. Here are some things we did together:

_____

_____

_____

_____

_____

_____

Here is a picture of my special stuffed animal or toy.

Art & Poetry Activities

Eggs

Supplies:

- large pieces of pink or light purple construction paper, one per student
- oval-shaped or rectangular sponges
- Cracked Egg Patterns (page 244)
- scissors
- 4–5 bright colors of water-base paint
- plastic or Styrofoam bowls
- "Eggs" poem and "April" title, one per student (top half of page 243)
- glue
- Favorite Memories, one per student (page 37)

Instructions:

Use the Cracked Egg Patterns to cut the sponges into the correct shapes for this activity.

Distribute the construction paper to students. Show youngsters how to dip a sponge into a bowl of paint and use it to make a print on the construction paper. Allow students to make egg prints on the construction paper. Encourage them to use a variety of paint colors. Allow the paint to dry.

Distribute the top half of page 243 to students. Read aloud the poem "Eggs" to the class. Have students cut out the poem and the "April" title and glue it onto the middle of the construction paper.

Distribute the Favorite Memories activity sheet to students. Help youngsters complete it. Then have students glue it onto the back of the construction paper.

Easter Time

Supplies:

- "Easter Time" poem and "April" title, one per student (bottom half of page 243)
- Bunny Puppet, one per student (page 245)
- scissors
- brown or white paper lunch bags, one per student
- glue
- Favorite Memories, one per student (page 37)

Instructions:

Give each student a copy of the bottom half of page 243, a Bunny Puppet, and a paper lunch bag. Tell students to cut the Bunny Puppet pieces. To make the puppet, tell students to turn the paper bag upside down without opening it. Show them how to glue the puppet's head onto the bottom of the bag. Then show them how to glue the puppet's front paws holding the egg and its back feet on the rest of the bag. Show them where the tail is glued on the back of the bag. Provide assistance as students make their own puppets. Read aloud the poem "Easter Time" to the class. Have students cut out the poem and "April" title and glue these onto the back of the paper bag bunny puppet. Teach students how to open and close the puppet's mouth as they recite the poem with you. If students have not already done a Favorite Memories activity sheet, help them complete one now. These can be displayed on a bulletin board or classroom wall.

April Poems

Eggs

Pretty eggs, what do you hide?

A sea turtle, lizard, or snake inside?

Pretty eggs, you make good homes.

What are you hiding under your domes?

Is it a chick or duck or bunny?

Is it something fuzzy or funny?

I guess we'll have to wait and see

Until the critter hatches free!

April

Easter Time

Easter time is finally here!

It's my favorite time of year.

Eggs and candy hidden here and there

In the grass and everywhere.

You can keep the eggs and candy, too,

Because for me, they just won't do!

The bunny is who I want to see,

But so far he's avoiding me!

April

Cracked Egg Patterns

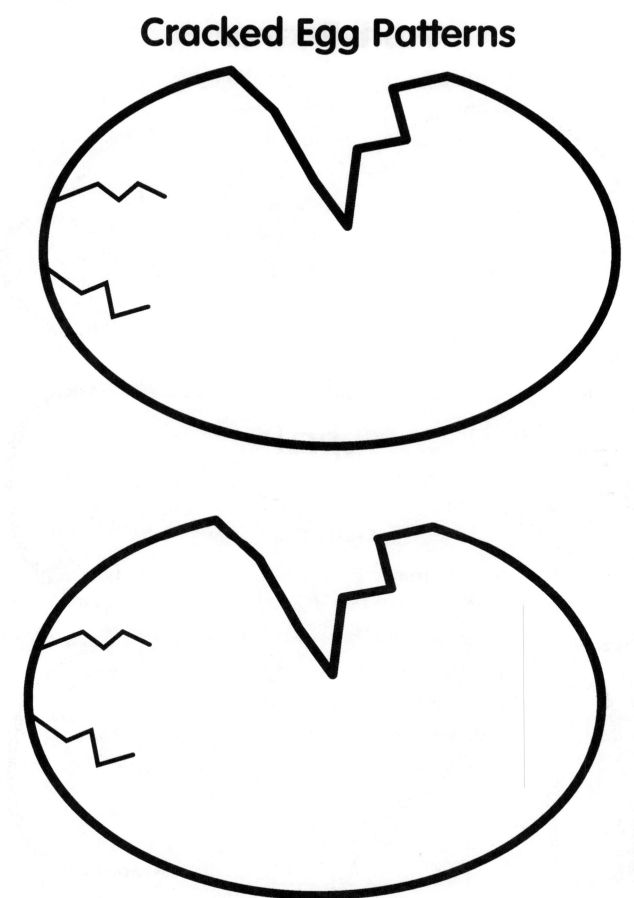

Bunny Puppet

I'm the Easter bunny!

Thematic Pins & Magnets

The Easter bunny magnet is fun for students to make on their own. Because of the size of this craft, it is easier to make the bunny into a magnetic gift rather than a pin. Using permanent markers instead of fabric paints makes this easier for children of all ages. Any type of design may be drawn on the egg that the Easter bunny is holding.

Instructions for the Easter bunny magnet are given below. Additional directions, as well as other ideas for materials to use when creating these gifts, are provided on page 9 of the How to Use Thematic Teaching Ideas section of this book.

Supplies:
- Easter Bunny pattern (below)
- pink vinyl
- scissors
- black, red, green, and purple fine-point permanent markers
- glue
- large magnetic strips, one per pattern

Instructions:
1. Have students trace the Easter Bunny pattern on to the pink vinyl.
2. Help students cut out the pink vinyl bunny.
3. Give students a variety of fine-point permanent markers to draw details on their vinyl bunnies.
4. Students may create an original design on the Easter Bunny's egg.
5. Help students glue a large magnetic strip onto the back of their vinyl bunny.

April Patterns

Easter Videotaping Ideas

The general directions for how to make a Class Video Book are on page 10 of the How to Use Thematic Teaching Ideas section of this book.

Allow time for students to learn and practice the song "Here Comes Peter Cottontail" (below). If you want students to act out the song as they are singing it, show them the actions that you would like for them to do.

Make a bunny ear headband for each student. First, cut two bunny ears out of pink construction paper. To make the headband, wrap the tagboard strip so it fits comfortably around a child's head. Carefully remove the headband from the child's head without changing the size. Staple the ends in place. Staple the bunny ears onto the headband. Use a black permanent marker to write the child's name across the headband. Then give the headband to the youngster. Ask students to wear their headbands while you are videotaping this part of the Class Video Book.

To introduce this April videotaping segment, use a stuffed bunny or bunny puppet. Have the bunny say, *Welcome to the month of April. Today is special because all my little bunny helpers are here today to sing a fun song about Easter. Here we go!*

Have students sing "Here Comes Peter Cottontail." You may wish to have the Bunny Puppet pretend it is leading the class as children sing the song.

Here Comes Peter Cottontail
(Traditional)

Here comes Peter Cottontail,
Hopping down the bunny trail,
Look at him stop, and listen to him say:

    "Try to do things you should."
    Maybe if you're extra good
    He'll roll lots of Easter eggs
    your way.

You'll wake up on Easter morning
And you'll know that he was there
When you find those chocolate bunnies
That he's hiding everywhere

Oh! Here comes Peter Cottontail,
Hopping down the bunny trail,
Happy, hoppity, Happy Easter Day.

After the class has sung "Here Comes Peter Cottontail," zoom in on students, one at a time, as you introduce them.

At the very end of this videotaping segment, have students look at the camera, smile, and say all together, *Happy Easter, Mom and Dad!*

May Themes:
Space and Occupations

Section Contents

Bibliography

Hopkins, T. *1001 Best Web Sites for Educators*. Teacher Created Materials, 2000. URL updates are available at the following address: http://www.teachercreated.com

Space

Berenstain, Stan and Jan. *The Berenstain Bears on the Moon*. Random House, 1987.

Cole, Joanna. *The Magic School Bus Lost in the Solar System*. Scholastic, 1992.

Hawcock, David. *The Amazing Pop-Up, Pull-Out Space Shuttle*. DK Publishing, 1998.

Jeunesse, Gallimard and Jean-Pierre Verdet. *The Earth and Sky (A First Discovery Book)*. Scholastic, 1992.

The Magic School Bus Out of this World. Videotape. Scholastic, Kid Vision, 1997. 30 minutes.

Rockwell, Anne F. and David Brion. *Space Vehicles*. Dutton Children's Books, 1994.

Sweeney, Joan. *Me and My Place in Space*. Crown, 1999.

Willis, Jeanne. *Earthlets, as Explained by Professor Xargle*. Dutton Children's Books, 1991.

http://www.spaceconnection.org This is the ultimate space Web site. It explores news about space, provides educational space activities for teachers and parents, explains what products we use here on Earth that originated in space, etc.

Occupations

Barrows, Allison. *The Artist's Friends*. Lerner, 1997.

Kuklin, Susan. *Fighting Fires*. Simon & Schuster Children's Books, 1999.

Maynard, Christopher. *Jobs People Do*. DK Publishing, 1997.

Merriam, Eve. *Daddies at Work*. Simon & Schuster Children's, 1996.

Merriam, Eve. *Mommies at Work*. Simon & Schuster Children's, 1996.

Activity Card #1

Activity Card #1: Astronaut Training — Obstacle Course

Supplies:

- plastic tape or wide masking tape
- gym mats
- three or four hula hoops
- one ladder
- one low balance beam
- one rebounder
- two chairs
- one short jump rope

Note: If any of the items listed above are not available, improvise by creating an obstacle course using desks, chairs, ropes, etc.

Instructions:

1. Put down gym mats where the obstacle course will be, so students will be protected if they fall.

2. Set up an obstacle course for students to move through. Below is an example of what an obstacle course might look like.

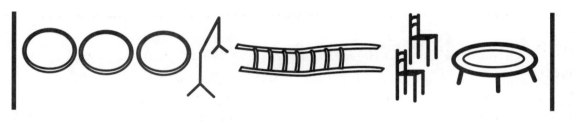

| Starting | Hula Hoops | Low Balance | Ladder | Chairs | Rebounder | Finish |
| Line | | Beam | | | | Line |

3. Use plastic tape or wide masking tape to mark the starting and finish lines of the obstacle course.

4. Explain to students the importance of astronauts staying fit when they are in training.

5. Point out the obstacle course to students.

6. Tell youngsters they will do warm-up exercises, then the obstacle course, and end with some cool-down exercises.

7. For the warm-up exercises, have students touch their toes 10 times with their legs straight, do 10 jumping jacks, and jog in place for 25 seconds.

8. Then have students go through the obstacle course, one at a time.

9. For the cool-down exercise, have students stretch as high as they can and gently bend from the waist to touch their toes. Have children do this 10 times.

10. Then have students take 5 balloon breaths by inhaling while raising their arms. As they exhale, have students lower their arms.

Extension: Encourage students to repeat the obstacle course two or three times. Then allow time for students to get a drink of water.

Activity Cards #2 and #3

Activity Card #2: Space Shuttles

Supplies:

- Space Shuttle, one for each student and one for demonstration (page 255)
- markers

Instructions:

1. Distribute the Space Shuttle activity sheet to students.

2. Demonstrate how to fold the activity sheet into a space shuttle. Help students fold their space shuttles.

3. Tell students to use markers to decorate their space shuttles.

Extension: Take students outside to fly their space shuttles.

Activity Card #3: Crayon Resist Space Art

Supplies:

- white art paper, one piece per student
- solar system poster
- crayons
- black watercolor paint
- plastic or Styrofoam bowls
- paintbrushes
- various colors of large construction paper, one piece per student
- glue

Instructions:

1. Show students a poster of our solar system. Point to each planet and name it. Explain that all the planets in our solar system revolve around the sun. Point out the sun.

2. Distribute the art paper to students. Have children color a picture of space using only crayons. Be sure students do not use black or brown crayons. Encourage youngsters to draw stars, the sun, a spaceship, planets, etc. Tell students to press extra hard when coloring to create a waxy buildup on their papers.

3. Have students paint over the artwork with black watercolor paint to complete their space pictures.

4. Allow the space crayon resist pictures to dry.

5. Frame each student's picture with a colorful piece of large construction paper.

Extension: Leave the center set up with the crayons, bowls of black watercolor paint, paintbrushes, and the solar system poster. Place more white art paper in the center. Ask students to create additional space pictures.

Activity Card #4

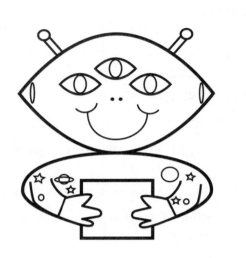

Activity Card #4: Space Alien Puppets

Supplies:

- Space Alien Puppet, one per student (page 256)
- small paper bags, one per student
- glue
- scissors
- crayons

Instructions:

1. Make a sample puppet to show students.

2. Read aloud the note that the puppet is holding.

3. Distribute the puppet activity sheets and the paper bags to students.

4. Have students color the puppet.

5. Tell students to cut out the puppet.

6. To put the puppet together, tell students to turn the paper bag upside down without opening it. Show them how to glue the puppet's head onto the bottom of the bag. Then show them how to glue the puppet's body below the head. Provide assistance as students make their own puppets.

7. Encourage students to draw fuzzy feet on the front of the paper bag.

8. Teach students how to open and close the puppet's mouth as youngsters talk.

Extension: Invite students to have the space alien puppets talk to each other. Encourage students to have their space aliens share information such as what planet they are from, what they eat, what games they like to play, and how they got to planet Earth.

Activity Card #5

Activity Card #5: Astronauts and Space Suitcases

Supplies:

- small paper plates, one per student
- Space Helmet Pattern (page 257)
- American flag stickers, one per student (optional)
- Astronauts one per student (page 258)
- Space Suitcase, one per student (page 259)
- scissors
- glue
- crayons or markers

Instructions:

1. Use the Space Helmet Pattern to cut the small paper plates into space helmets. Cut out part of the middle section for the faceplate of the helmet. You may wish to add an American flag sticker above the center of the faceplate.

2. Tell students that they will be making astronaut paper dolls. Distribute the paper plate space helmets, the astronauts, and the Space Suitcase activity sheets to students.

3. Have students color the astronauts, drawing their own faces inside the helmets.

4. Have youngsters cut out the astronauts and glue the paper plate space helmets onto the paper dolls.

5. On the Space Suitcase activity sheet, have students list several things they would take with them when visiting outer space. Students may list food items, photographs of family members, special toys, etc.

6. Have students cut out the Space Suitcase and glue it between the Astronaut paper doll's hands.

7. Allow the glue to dry.

Extension: Obtain some toy astronauts and spacecrafts. Place these in a center with a variety of blocks. Encourage students to create space stations, using the wooden blocks and toy astronauts and spacecrafts.

Award Certificate

Give students the Space's Special Day Award Certificate after they have completed all five center activities. You may prefer to fill in individual student names ahead of time.

✂ -

Congratulations to _____

for completing the

Space's Special Day Centers!

_____   _____
          Teacher   Date

✂ -

Congratulations to _____

for completing the

Space's Special Day Centers!

_____   _____
          Teacher   Date

Space Shuttle Pattern

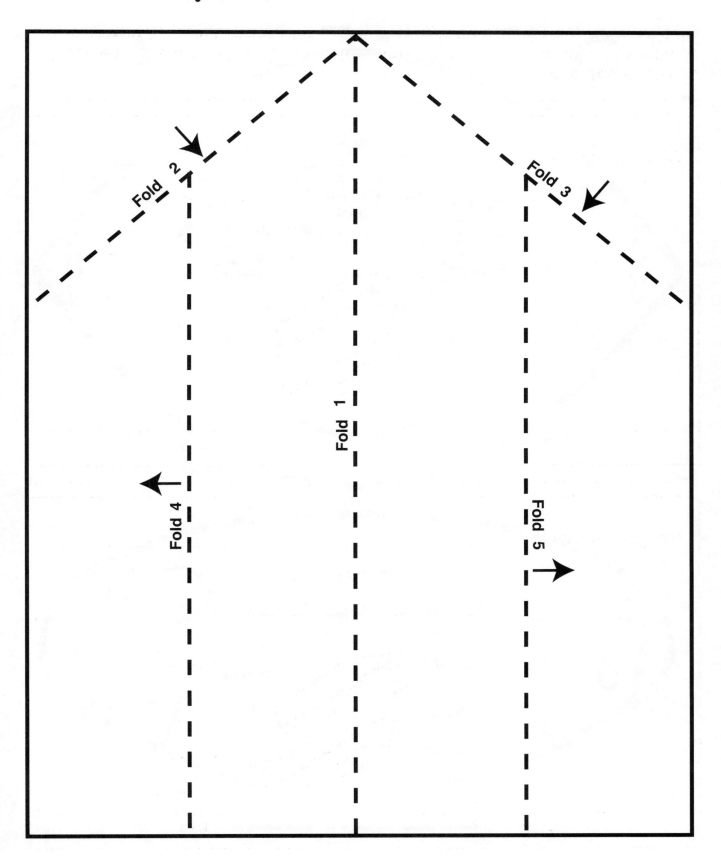

Space Alien Puppet

I am a little space alien who is visiting your classroom. My name is Fuzzy Feet.

Space Helmet Pattern

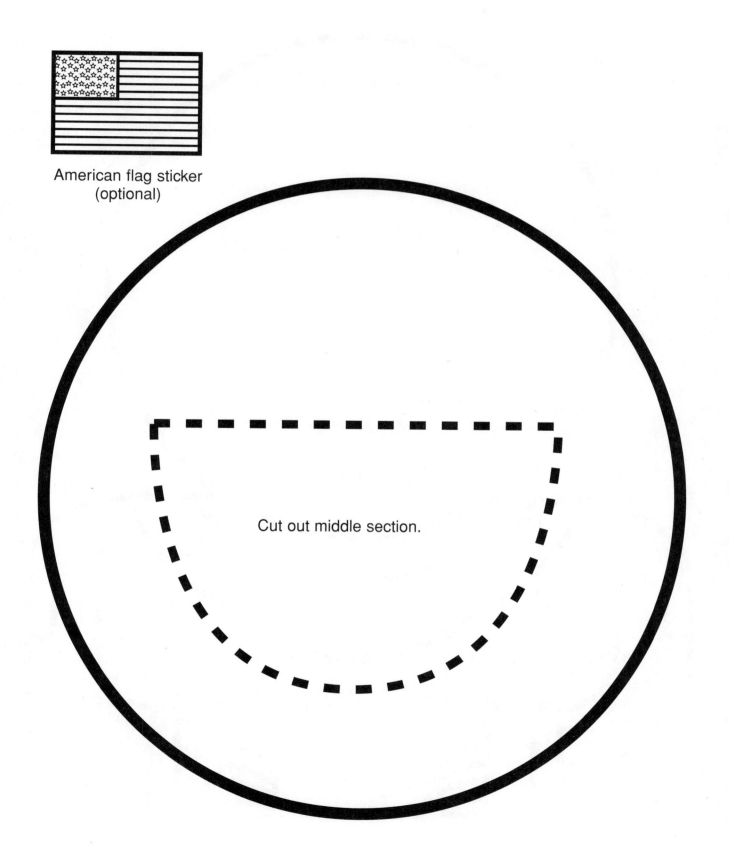

American flag sticker
(optional)

Cut out middle section.

Astronaut

(Glue helmet here.)

(Glue space
suitcase handle
here.)

Space Suitcase

Write a story and then cut the suitcase out and glue it to the astronaut on page 258.

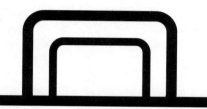

In my space suitcase, I will take _____

_____

_____

_____

_____

_____

_____

Snack Ideas and Recommended Book

Supplies:
- plain white napkins
- star stickers
- star-shaped cookies, two per student
- canned frosting
- cookie decorations such as colored sprinkles and small candies
- small paper plates, one per student
- plastic knives, one per student
- milk or juice
- plastic or paper cups, one per student

WARNING: Be sure to ask parents if their children have any food allergies or dietary restrictions before using the following snack idea.

Instructions:
After students have completed all five centers, give each student a plain white napkin and some star stickers. Invite youngsters to decorate the napkin using the star stickers.

Then give each student a paper plate with two star-shaped sugar cookies, some frosting, and cookie decorations such as colored sprinkles and small candies. In addition, give each student a plastic knife.

plastic knife

frosting

cookies

sprinkles/candies

Tell students to use the knife to spread the frosting on the cookie. Then invite students to decorate their cookies with sprinkles, candies, etc.

After students have decorated their cookies, give each child a cup of milk or juice. Then invite students to eat their cookies and drink their beverages.

Recommended Book: On Space's Special Day, read aloud *Earthlets, as Explained by Professor Xargle* by Jeanne Willis (Dutton Children's Books, 1991). This is a hilarious fiction story about space aliens visiting Earth. The aliens label many ordinary human items with funny names and purposes. The book is very entertaining for a young audience.

Occupations Whole Class Activity

Supplies:

- *Jobs People Do* by Christopher Maynard (DK Publishing, 1997)
- When I Grow Up, one per student (page 262)
- Parent Letter, one per student (page 263)
- pencils
- crayons or markers
- large piece of construction paper, one per student

Instructions:

Read aloud the book *Jobs People Do* by Christopher Maynard. Discuss with students the various occupations shown in the book. Have students tell what occupations they would like to have when they grow up.

Distribute the copies of the When I Grow Up activity sheet. Help students fill in the blanks on the activity sheet. Then ask youngsters to draw pictures of themselves doing the types of job they want as adults.

Give each student a piece of large construction paper. You may wish to allow students to pick their favorite color of large construction paper. Use the large construction paper to mount the When I Grow Up activity sheets. Then display the activity sheets on a bulletin board or a classroom wall.

Next ask students to play an occupational guessing game. Invite youngsters to take turns acting out their future occupations. Allow the rest of the class to guess what job is being acted out. Be sure all students have an opportunity to act out their future occupations.

Reproduce the Parent Letter to send home with students. In the letter, parents are invited to visit your classroom to tell about their occupations. The letter tells parents about how long their presentation should last and suggests ideas about bringing hands-on objects from the workplace to help hold a young audience's attention.

Times are arranged so parents can come in and share their occupations on alternating days. It is recommended that only one or two presentations be given per day. If you know ahead of time the parent occupations for the day, you may wish to share some related children's books with the class in preparation for the visitors.

When I Grow Up

Name: _____ Date: _____

When I grow up I want to be a _____ because

_____

_____

_____

_____

_____ .

Here I am all grown up!

Parent Letter

Dear Parent:

This month, our class is learning about different occupations. We would like to invite you to come to school to tell about your occupation.

If you would like to share information about your occupation, please prepare a presentation that is 15–20 minutes long. Children would enjoy seeing real tools and materials that you use for your job. For example, you could bring small machines, brochures, or special pencils to show students.

If you are interested in being a guest speaker for our class, please fill out the form at the bottom of the page and return it to me as soon as possible. Then I will call you to arrange a date and time for your presentation.

We look forward to hearing from you and hope that you have time to tell us about your occupation. Please feel free to call me if you have any questions.

Sincerely,

_____

Teacher

_____

Phone Number

- -

Please return this form as soon as possible.

Child's name: _____

Parent's name: _____

Parent's occupation: _____

Phone number: _____

Circle best day for presentation:

Monday   Tuesday   Wednesday   Thursday   Friday

Thank you!

Buddy Time Activities

Space Alien Information

Reproduce the Space Alien Information form (page 265). For a prewriting activity, have students name planets in our solar system, list words describing space aliens, name different types of foods aliens might eat, etc. Refer to a copy of the information form as you conduct this brainstorming activity. As students generate ideas, write their suggestions on a white board or chalkboard. After brainstorming, tell the big buddies to help their little buddies fill in the blanks on the information form. Remind youngsters to use their imaginations as they complete the form. Have the buddies work together to draw a picture of the space alien with its best friend at the bottom of the form.

Occupations

Reproduce the Occupations activity sheet (page 266) for the big and little buddies. Have the big buddies help the little buddies fill in the blanks at the top of the activity sheet. Then have the little buddies draw a picture of themselves to show what kind of clothes they might wear when doing the job they want to do as adults. You may wish to have occupational posters or books available for students to preview before completing this activity.

What I Want to Be

Reproduce the poem "What I Want to Be" (page 267) and the Poem Art activity sheet (page 268). Cut apart the copies of the poem. Give one copy of the poem to each pair of buddies. Read aloud the poem. Have the buddies glue the poem onto the back of the Poem Art activity sheet. Then ask the buddies to illustrate the Poem Art by using crayons or markers to draw pictures of the sky, a plane, a mouse, a haunted house, and something furry, rough, and wild. Ask the big buddies to read the poem to their little buddies several more times. Then encourage the little buddies to take home the poem and artwork to share with their families.

Space Alien Information

Date: _____

Little Buddy's Name: _____

Big Buddy's Name: _____

I am a space alien from the planet _____ .

My name is _____ . On my planet we eat _____

and drink _____ .

I have two antennas. I use my antennas for _____ .

I have three eyes. I use my eyes to _____ .

I am green because _____ .

My feet have claws, so I can _____ .

For fun, sometimes I like to _____ .

For transportation, I drive _____ .

If I could go anywhere on planet Earth, I would go to _____

because _____ .

My best friend's name is _____ .

My best friend is from the planet _____ .

Here is a picture of me with my best friend.

```




```

Occupations

Date: _____

Little Buddy's Name: _____

Big Buddy's Name: _____

When I grow up, I want to be a _____

because _____

_____.

Here is a picture of me as a grown-up, wearing the kind of clothes I might need to wear when doing my job.

Poem

What I Want to Be
(Author Unknown)

People always say to me, "What do you think you'd like to be when you grow up?"

And I say, "Why, I think I'd like to be the sky or a plane or a mouse or maybe a haunted house . . .

Or something furry, rough, and wild, or maybe I will stay a child!"

What I Want to Be
(Author Unknown)

People always say to me, "What do you think you'd like to be when you grow up?"

And I say, "Why, I think I'd like to be the sky or a plane or a mouse or maybe a haunted house . . .

Or something furry, rough, and wild, or maybe I will stay a child!"

What I Want to Be
(Author Unknown)

People always say to me, "What do you think you'd like to be when you grow up?"

And I say, "Why, I think I'd like to be the sky or a plane or a mouse or maybe a haunted house . . .

Or something furry, rough, and wild, or maybe I will stay a child!"

What I Want to Be
(Author Unknown)

People always say to me, "What do you think you'd like to be when you grow up?"

And I say, "Why, I think I'd like to be the sky or a plane or a mouse or maybe a haunted house . . .

Or something furry, rough, and wild, or maybe I will stay a child!"

Poem Art

Sky	Plane
Mouse	**Haunted House**
Something Furry, Rough, and Wild	

Space Bear Backpack Buddy

May Theme: Space

Backpack Buddy: small bear wearing an astronaut suit

Storybook: *Me and My Place in Space* by Joan Sweeney and illustrated by Annette Cable (Crown Publishing Group, 1999)

Supplies:
- journal
- Letter from Space Bear Backpack Buddy (page 270)
- Journal Assignment, one per student (page 271)
- backpack
- Space Bear Backpack Buddy

Instructions:

You may wish to make the writing journals from portfolios with fasteners. Be sure there are enough journal pages (copies of page 271) for every student in the classroom to complete the writing assignment. Also place a copy of the Letter from Space Bear Backpack Buddy inside the journal. The homework assignment is described for parents and students in this letter. However, you may prefer to explain the assignment to students before they take it home.

For this journal assignment, students read the book *Me and My Place in Space.* Then they draw a pictures of themselves and the space bear in a spacecraft. They also write about some of the things they did while on a space adventure with the space bear.

Before sending the backpack home with a different child each day, check to be sure it has the small bear wearing an astronaut suit, the book *Me and My Place in Space,* and the writing journal. Remind the student who is taking these materials home to return the backpack and its contents the next school day. When it is the next school day, allow time for the student who took the backpack home to share his/her journal writing assignment with the class.

Be sure every student has an opportunity to take the backpack home. After all students have completed the writing assignment, make the journal a permanent addition to your classroom library.

Letter from Space Bear Backpack Buddy

Dear Friend,

I am a little astronaut bear named Star. I am looking forward to spending the night with you and your family. During my visit, I would like for you and your parents to read the space book *Me and My Place in Space* by Joan Sweeney. You will find this book in my backpack. It's one of my favorites.

After you read *Me and My Place in Space,* use your imagination to pretend that you and I are on a spacecraft traveling in outer space. Then please use a page in this journal to draw a picture of us in our spacecraft and to write about some of the things that happened while we were on our space adventure.

I can't wait to travel with you into outer space!

Your friend,

Star the Space Bear

P.S. Please don't forget to put the book *Me and My Place in Space,* this journal, and me inside the backpack and return all these things to your teacher. You will get to share your writing assignment with the class, and another student will get to take me home.

Journal Assignment

Name: _____ Date: _____

Here is a picture of Star the Space Bear and me in our spacecraft. If you look closely, you can see our faces in the window of the spacecraft.

Here are some of the things that happened while Star and I were on our space adventure.

_____

_____

_____

_____

_____

We had a great time! I hope Star can come visit me again some day.

Art & Poetry Activities

UFO

Supplies:

- white construction paper, one piece per student
- "UFO" poem and "May" title, one per student (top half of page 273)
- UFO Picture, one per student (page 274)
- crayons or markers
- scissors
- glue
- small photo of each student from the waist up
- black watercolor paint
- plastic or Styrofoam bowls
- paintbrushes
- large piece of dark blue construction paper, one per student
- Favorite Memories, one per student (page 37)

Instructions:

Distribute the white construction paper, as well as the copies of the UFO Picture and the top half of page 273. Have students color and cut out the UFO Picture. Help students glue a photograph of themselves inside a window of the UFO. Ask students to use the crayons or markers to draw outer space pictures, such as stars, planets, moons, the sun, space aliens, and meteorites, on the white construction paper. Be sure students do not use black or brown crayons. Tell youngsters to press extra hard when coloring to create a waxy buildup on their papers. Then have students cover their crayon pictures with black watercolor paint. When the paint is dry, have students glue their UFO Pictures onto the white construction paper. Next have them glue the white construction paper, the poem "UFO," and the "May" title onto the blue construction paper. Read aloud the poem "UFO." Distribute the Favorite Memories activity sheet. Help students fill it out. Then have youngsters glue it onto the back of the blue construction paper.

Occupations

Supplies:

- "Occupations" poem and "May" title, one per student (bottom half of page 273)
- Paper Doll, one per student (page 275)
- fabric or construction paper scraps
- scissors
- glue
- markers or crayons
- large piece of red construction paper, one per student
- Favorite Memories, one per student (page 37)

Instructions:

Distribute the materials listed above. Have students fill in the blanks on the Paper Doll activity sheet. Tell children to glue fabric or construction paper clothes on the paper doll. Explain that they should show clothes on the paper doll that represent the kind of outfit they will wear when they go to work as an adult. Have students use markers or crayons to add details (facial features, hair, etc.) to the paper doll. Ask students to glue the Paper Doll activity sheet, "Occupations" poem, and "May" title onto a piece of large red construction paper. Read aloud the poem to the class. If students have not already done a Favorite Memories activity sheet, help them complete one now. Tell them to glue it onto the back of the red construction paper.

May Poems

UFO

Here I am in my UFO

Trying not to fly too low.

The stars are bright and so is the moon.

I should be back on Earth real soon.

It's the pretty blue planet in the sky.

Oops! The little blue dot I just flew by.

But I'll solve this problem, have no fear—

A turn-around place must be near.

Maybe I'll fly through this big black hole.

Oops! Good-bye to the world I used to knowwwww!

Occupations

(Author Unknown)

People always say to me,

"What do you think you'd like to be when you grow up?"

And I say, "Why, I think I'd like to be the sky or a plane or a mouse or maybe a haunted house . . .

Or something furry, rough, and wild, or maybe I will stay a child!"

UFO Picture

Paper Doll

Name: _____ Date: _____

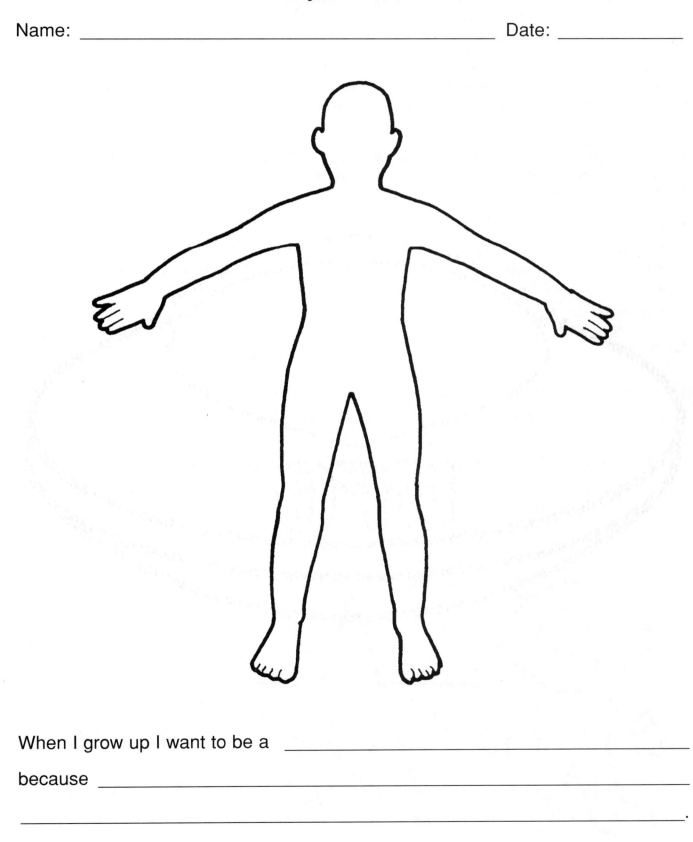

When I grow up I want to be a _____

because _____

_____.

Thematic Pins & Magnets

Space is a fun unit of study for children of all ages. A friendly space alien magnet or pin (below) makes the perfect gift to correspond to this unit. Other space patterns are available below and on page 277. Use any patterns that are appropriate for your students.

The astronaut (below) is a popular magnet/pin with children. The unique characteristic about this magnet/pin is the face. You glue a photograph of the student's face inside the helmet. Then you can use liquid embroidery paint or permanent markers to write the name of the student on the front of the astronaut suit.

Instructions for the space alien magnet/pin are given below. Additional directions, as well as other ideas for materials to use when creating these gifts, are provided on page 9 of the How to Use Thematic Teaching Ideas section of this book.

Supplies:

- space alien pattern (below)
- black permanent marker
- heart-shaped plastic jewel, one per pattern
- magnetic strip or pin, one per pattern
- yellow vinyl
- green and blue liquid embroidery paint
- glue
- scissors

Instructions:

1. Have students trace the space alien pattern onto the green vinyl and then cut it out.

2. Tell students to use the black markers to draw the details on the vinyl space alien.

3. Ask students to use the liquid embroidery paint to color the vinyl space alien's antennas dark green and its eyes blue.

4. Help students glue on the heart jewel so it is centered under the space alien's neck.

5. Then tell students to glue a magnetic strip or a pin onto the back of the vinyl space alien. Provide assistance as needed.

May Patterns

Space Videotaping Ideas

The general directions for how to make a Class Video Book are on page 10 of the How to Use Thematic Teaching Ideas section of this book.

Allow time for students to learn and practice the poem "UFO" (below). Teach students how to recite the poem with dramatic expression and use hand and body motions to make the actions described in the poem come alive.

UFO

Here I am in my UFO

Trying not to fly too low.

The stars are bright and so is the moon.

I should be back on Earth real soon.

It's the pretty blue planet in the sky.

Oops! The little blue dot I just flew by.

But I'll solve this problem, I'll have no fear.

A turn-around place must be near.

Maybe I'll fly through this big black hole.

Oops! Good-bye to the world I use to knowwwww!

Review with students the things they listed on their space suitcases (page 259) for Activity Card #5.

Begin this month's videotaping segment by making the following announcement: *During the month of May, the students in our class have been astronauts traveling in outer space. Today these astronauts would like to recite a special poem entitled "UFO."* Videotape students reciting the poem "UFO."

After the class recites the poem together, zoom the camera in on individual students. Introduce each student as Astronaut _____ (Insert the student's name in the blank). Next ask student astronauts to name two or three things they packed in their space suitcases (page 259) for their journey in space.

At the very end of this videotaping segment, encourage student astronauts to look at the camera, wave, and say all together, *See you back on planet Earth, Mom and Dad!*

June Themes:
Teddy Bears and Real Bears

Section Contents

Bibliography

Hopkins, T. *1001 Best Web Sites for Educators.* Teacher Created Materials, 2000. URL updates are available at the following address: http://www.teachercreated.com

Teddy Bears

Alborough, Jez. *Where's My Teddy?* Candlewick Press, 1994.

Berenstain, Stan and Jan. *The Bears' Vacation.* Beginner Books, 1976.

Berenstain Bears Too Much Birthday. Videotape. Random House, 1985. 30 minutes.

Carlstrom, Nancy White. *Jesse Bear, What Will You Wear?* Simon & Schuster Children's, 1996.

De Beer, Hans. *Ahoy There, Little Polar Bear.* North South Books, 1997.

Freeman, Don. *Corduroy.* Penguin Putnam Books for Young Readers, 1988.

Galdone, Paul (editor). *The Three Bears.* Houghton Mifflin, 1985.

Gliori, Debi. *Mr. Bear Babysits.* Western, 1994.

Waber, Bernard. *Ira Sleeps Over.* Houghton Mifflin, 1989.

Waddell, Martin. *You and Me, Little Bear.* Candlewick Press, 1998.

Real Bears

Buxton, Jane Heath. *Baby Bears and How They Grow.* National Geographic Society, 1986. (Out of print)

Gilks, Helen. *Bears.* Ticknor and Fields, 1993.

Markle, Sandra. *Growing Up Wild: Bears.* Simon & Schuster Children's, 2000.

Petty, Kate. *Bears.* Barron's Educational Series, 1992.

Tasha the Polar Bear. Videotape. National Geographic Kids' Video, 1998. 30 minutes.

Activity Cards #1 and #2

Activity Card #1: Teddy Bear Measurement

Supplies:

- small to medium-sized teddy bears, one per student
- 50–100 plastic Unifix™ cubes
- Teddy Bear Measurement, one per student (page 285)

Instructions:

1. Ahead of time, send a note home asking parents to send a small to medium-sized teddy bear to school with their children on a date that you specify. Be sure to have some extra teddy bears on hand for students who forget theirs.

2. Invite students to bring their teddy bears to the center to be measured. Provide a teddy bear to any student who does not have one.

3. First encourage students to tell about their bears.

4. Distribute the Teddy Bear Measurement activity sheet to student and read it aloud.

5. Have students use the Unifix® cubes to measure the various parts of their teddy bears. Ask them to use the activity sheet to record the number of cubes it takes to measure each part. For younger students, you may wish to write the numbers on their activity sheets.

6. Ask students to draw a picture of themselves with their teddy bears.

Extension: Suggest to students that they use the Unifix cubes to measure their own arms, hands, fingers, legs, and feet.

Activity Card #2: My Teddy Bear Story

Supplies:

- small to medium-sized teddy bear, one per student
- My Teddy Bear Story, one per student (page 286)
- pencils
- art paper, one piece per student
- markers or crayons

Instructions:

1. If you have not already done so, send a note home asking parents to send a small to medium-sized teddy bear to school with their children on a date that you specify. Be sure to have some extra teddy bears on hand for students who forget theirs.

2. Ask students the following questions about their bears: *What is your bear's name? Where or how did you get your bear? Why do you like your bear?*

3. Distribute the My Teddy Bear Story activity sheet and art paper to students. Have older students fill in the blanks of the activity sheet by themselves. Allow younger students to dictate their responses for you to write on the activity sheet.

4. After students complete the activity sheet, ask children to use the crayons or markers to draw a portrait of their teddy bears on the art paper.

Extension: Ask students to draw families for their teddy bears.

Activity Card #3

Activity Card #3: Teddy Bear Games

Supplies:

- small to medium-sized teddy bear one per student,
- small parachute
- tape measure (optional)
- teddy bear stickers (optional)

WARNING: Allow plenty of space, such as a playground or gym, for this activity.

Instructions:

1. If you have not already done so, send a note home asking parents to send a small to medium-sized teddy bear to school with their children on a date that you specify. Be sure to have some extra teddy bears on hand for students who forget theirs.

2. Have students play Teddy Bear Toss with a partner. In this game, two students stand approximately 4–6 feet (1.2–2.4 m) apart from each other. They use an underhanded throw to toss a teddy bear back and forth to one another. Tell the partners to use one student's bear and then the other student's bear. Have students count how many times they can catch each bear.

3. Have students play the Teddy Bear Parachute Game. For this game, spread the parachute out on the ground and place one small teddy bear in the middle of the parachute. Have students stand in a circle around the parachute, grab onto the edges of the parachute, and lift the parachute and teddy bear off the ground. Ask students to move their arms up and down, while holding the edges of the parachute, to bounce the teddy bear. Encourage students to keep bouncing the teddy bear until it is tossed off the parachute.

4. Have students play the Teddy Bear Merry-Go-Round Game. For this game, spread the parachute out on the ground and place one small teddy bear in the middle of the parachute. Have students stand in a circle around the parachute, grab onto the edges of the parachute, and lift the parachute and teddy bear off the ground. Ask students to turn so that only their right hands are holding the parachute. Explain that they are going to be like a merry-go-round at an amusement park. Tell students to give the teddy bear a ride on the merry-go-round by walking clockwise in a circle. Remind students that they should continue to hold on to the parachute with their right hands as they walk around in a circle.

5. Ask students to play the Teddy Bear Throwing Contest. **Note:** Do not allow students to throw teddy bears that look worn out or fragile in any way. To play this game, have students line up with their teddy bears. One at a time, ask children to throw their bears as far as they can. Be sure all students throw from the same starting point. Use a tape measure to determine who threw a teddy bear the farthest.

Extension: Collect a variety of books about bears. Invite students to read and enjoy the books.

Activity Card #4

Activity Card #4: Teddy Bear Mobiles

Supplies:

- Teddy Bear Mobile (page 287)
- tan or brown construction paper, one piece per student
- scissors
- crayons or markers
- bow tie ribbons, various colors and sizes
- a wide variety of buttons
- glue
- yarn, one piece per student
- hole puncher

Instructions:

1. Ahead of time, reproduce the Teddy Bear Mobile on tan or brown construction paper.

2. Distribute the construction paper teddy bears to students. Tell students to cut out the construction paper teddy bears.

3. Ask youngsters to use markers or crayons to color the eyes, face, vest, etc.

4. Invite students to glue ribbon bow ties and vest buttons on the construction paper teddy bears. Allow the glue to dry.

5. Help students punch a hole at the top of their construction paper teddy bears.

6. For each bear, string a piece of yarn through the hole you have punched. Tie the yarn onto the bear, or make a loop with the yarn and tie the two ends together.

7. Display the construction paper teddy bears in the classroom. As an alternative, you may wish to encourage youngsters to hang their construction paper teddy bears at home.

Extension: Have students sort and count the extra buttons at this center.

Activity Card #5

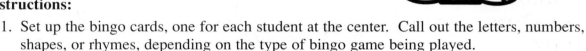

Activity Card #5: Teddy Bear Bingo

Supplies:

- small plastic teddy bear counters
- one or more primary bingo games: ABC Bingo, Number Bingo, Shape Bingo, Rhyming Bingo
- teddy bear stickers (optional)

Instructions:

1. Set up the bingo cards, one for each student at the center. Call out the letters, numbers, shapes, or rhymes, depending on the type of bingo game being played.

2. As you call out each bingo item (letter, number, shape, or rhyme), have students use their teddy bear counters to cover the appropriate squares on their bingo cards.

3. When students completely cover one row, they should say, *Bingo!* You may wish to give stickers to the winning students or to all students for participating.

4. You may wish to have students play blackout bingo, for which the object of the game is to fill up all the spaces on the bingo card. Once again have students use plastic teddy bears as the markers on their bingo cards.

Extension: Play several different games of bingo with students. Children usually enjoy this very much.

Award Certificate

Give students the Teddy Bears' Special Day Award Certificate after they have completed all five center activities. You may prefer to fill in individual student names ahead of time.

✂ --

Congratulations to _____

for completing the

Teddy Bears' Special Day Centers!

_____   _____
Teacher   Date

✂ --

Congratulations to _____

for completing the

Teddy Bears' Special Day Centers!

_____   _____
Teacher   Date

Teddy Bear Measurement

Name: _____ Date: _____

My teddy bear's name is _____ .

Here are some of my teddy bear's measurements.

Arm _____

Leg _____

Head (across from side to side) _____

Length (from foot to top of head) _____

Width (across the tummy) _____

Here is a picture of me with my teddy bear.

I love my teddy bear!

My Teddy Bear Story

Name: _____ Date: _____

My teddy bear's name is _____ .

My teddy bear and I love to travel together. This time we are traveling

to _____ .

We will be taking a _____ to get there.

This is what is in my teddy bear's suitcase.

_____, Suitcase

List of Items   **Pictures of Items**

1. _____

2. _____

3. _____

One of our favorite things to do when we are traveling together is to

_____ .

Our favorite foods are _____ .

Next time my teddy bear and I travel, we plan to go to _____

because _____ .

Teddy Bear Mobile

Snack Ideas and Recommended Book

Supplies:

- refrigerated quick biscuit dough
- teddy bear shaped cookie cutter
- stove or toaster oven (optional)
- baking tray (optional)
- oven mitts (optional)
- spatula (optional)
- paper plates, one per student

- small paper bowls, one per student
- berries such as strawberries, raspberries, and blueberries
- whipped cream
- juice or milk (optional)
- plastic or paper cups (optional)
- picnic blankets (optional)

WARNINGS: Be sure to ask parents if their children have any food allergies or dietary restrictions. If you bake the biscuits in class, do not allow children near the hot stove or toaster oven.

Instructions:

Use the cookie cutter to make teddy bear shaped biscuits. You may wish to bake the biscuits at home and bring them to school rather than baking them in class. Allow the biscuits to cool before serving them to students on paper plates. Use small paper bowls to serve students some berries such as strawberries, raspberries, blueberries, or a mixture of all three. Top the berries with a small amount of whipped cream.

You may wish to serve students cups of milk or juice. To make the occasion more festive, children and their teddy bears could eat these snacks on picnic blankets either outside or inside the classroom, depending on the weather. While students eat their snacks, read aloud a favorite teddy bear story.

As an alternative, use the following snack suggestion.

Supplies:

- teddy bear shaped graham crackers
- gummy bears
- paper plates, one per student
- grapes
- juice
- plastic or paper cups, one per student

Instructions:

Serve students some teddy bear-shaped graham crackers, gummy bears, and grapes on paper plates. In addition, give each youngster a cup of juice. You may wish to take students and their teddies on a picnic to eat these snacks.

Recommended Book: On Teddy Bears' Special Day, read aloud *The Teddy Bears' Picnic* written by Bruce Whatley (HarperCollins Publishers, 1998). This is a fun book because it also includes teddy bear songs by Jerry Garcia and David Grisman.

Real Bears Whole Class Activity

Supplies:

- *Baby Bears and How They Grow* by Jane Heath Buxton (National Geographic Society, 1986; out of print)
- large white board or chalkboard
- teddy bear and real bear pictures (below)

- cellophane tape or double stick tape
- Teddy Bears, one per student (page 290)
- Real Bears, one per student (page 291)
- pencils
- crayons

Instructions:

Read aloud the special National Geographic children's book entitled *Baby Bears and How They Grow.* Show students the photographs as you read the book. After sharing the story, discuss with students the stages of a real bear's life and how it grows.

Enlarge the pictures of a teddy bear and real bear provided below. Make a two-column chart on the white board or chalkboard. At the top of one column, tape the picture of a teddy bear. At the top of the other column, tape the picture of a real bear.

Have students brainstorm the attributes of teddy bears and the attributes of real bears. Jot down students' comments in the appropriate columns.

Distribute the Teddy Bears and Real Bears activity sheets to students. Tell students that they may refer to the chart on the board while completing these activity sheets. On the Teddy Bears activity sheet, have youngsters draw pictures and write words and phrases that describe teddy bears. On the Real Bears activity sheet, have students draw pictures and write words and phrases that describe real bears. For example, students could draw a picture of bear claws on the Real Bears activity sheet. If children are old enough to write, ask them to print the word *claws* next to their pictures.

Collect and sort the two activity sheets so you can make two separate class books — one entitled *Teddy Bears* and the other entitled *Real Bears.* Share the books with the class. Then place them in your classroom library.

Teddy Bears

Name: _____ Date: _____

Real Bears

Name: _____ Date: _____

Buddy Time Activities

Teddy Bear Story

Invite the little buddies to bring a small to medium-sized teddy bear to school with them. Have some extra teddy bears on hand for students who forget theirs. When the big buddies arrive, distribute the My Teddy Bear activity sheet (page 293). Give each pair of buddies one copy. Ask the big buddies to help their little buddies fill in the blanks on the activity sheet to complete the imaginary story about their teddy bears. After the story is completed, give each pair of buddies a piece of white construction paper. Invite the buddies to draw a portrait of the little buddies' teddy bears. When the buddies are done with the picture, use tape or staples to attach the white construction paper to the activity sheet.

Three Bear Puppets

Read aloud two or three different versions of the story *The Three Bears* to the buddies. Have students compare and contrast the different versions of the story. Distribute copies of the Goldilocks and the Three Bears puppets (page 294) to the buddies. Tell the big buddies to help their little buddies make the puppets. Encourage the buddies to work together to color and cut out the puppets. Then help youngsters tape the puppets to straws or craft sticks. Ask the buddies to retell the three bears' story while using the puppets. Provide plain white envelopes for the little buddies to store their puppets. When this buddy project is completed, encourage the little buddies to take the puppets home to share with their families.

Summer Bookmarks

Reproduce the Summer Bookmarks (page 295) on cardstock. As an alternative, you can reproduce the bookmarks on paper and glue them onto strips of tagboard. Obtain some bear books for the big buddies to read to their little buddies. Cut the bookmarks apart. Give the bookmarks without a picture to the big buddies. Ask the big buddies to draw their own bears on their bookmarks. Give the bookmarks with the picture of the teddy bear to the little buddies. Ask the little buddies to trace and color the bears on their bookmarks. Have the buddies cut out their bookmarks. Laminate the bookmarks. Then allow the buddies to exchange bookmarks as special gifts.

My Teddy Bear

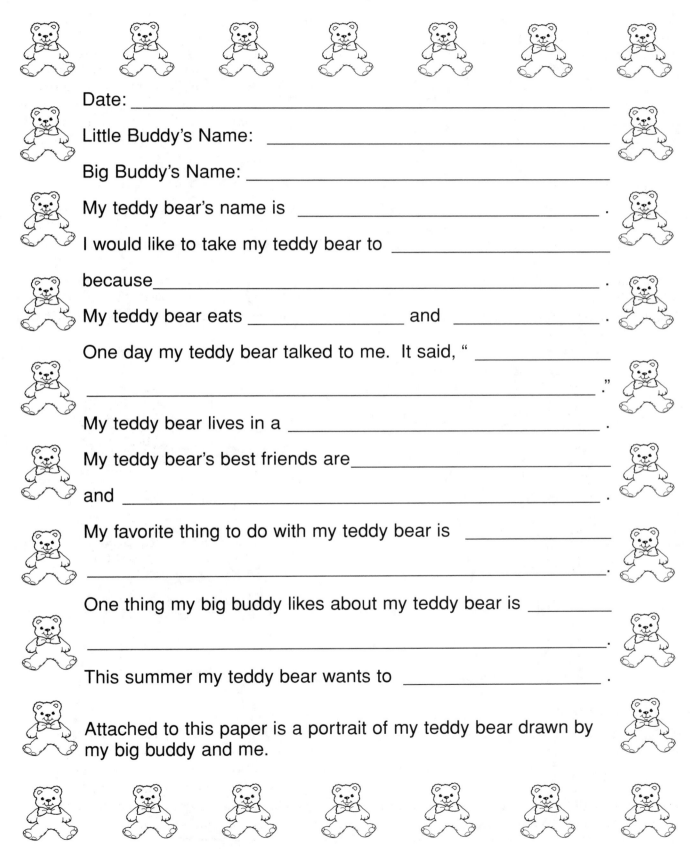

Date: _____

Little Buddy's Name: _____

Big Buddy's Name: _____

My teddy bear's name is _____ .

I would like to take my teddy bear to _____

because_____ .

My teddy bear eats _____ and _____ .

One day my teddy bear talked to me. It said, " _____

_____ ."

My teddy bear lives in a _____ .

My teddy bear's best friends are_____

and _____ .

My favorite thing to do with my teddy bear is _____

_____ .

One thing my big buddy likes about my teddy bear is _____

_____ .

This summer my teddy bear wants to _____ .

Attached to this paper is a portrait of my teddy bear drawn by my big buddy and me.

Goldilocks and the Three Bears

Mama Bear

Papa Bear

Baby Bear

Goldilocks

Summer Bookmarks

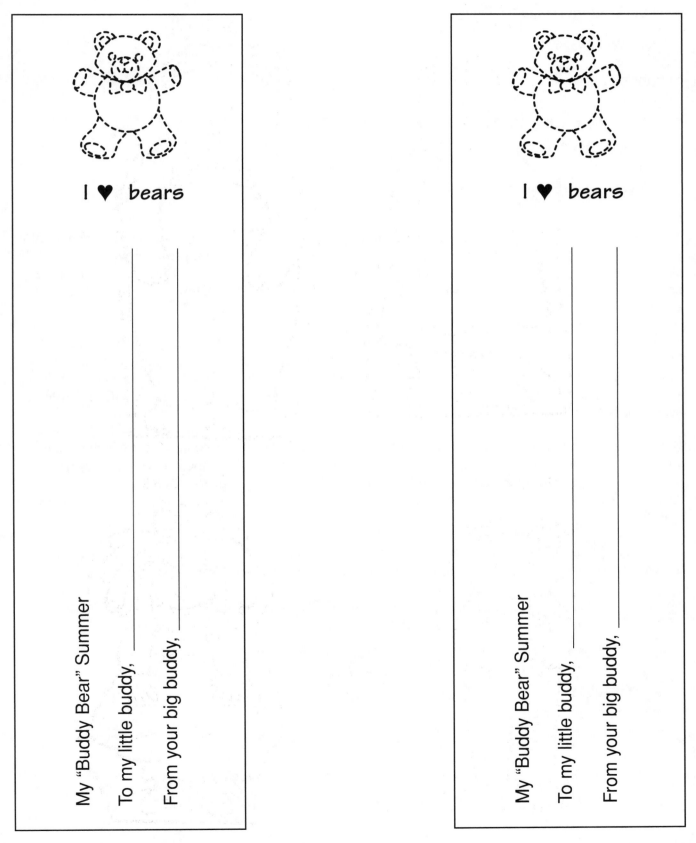

I ♥ bears

My "Buddy Bear" Summer

To my little buddy,

From your big buddy,

I ♥ bears

My "Buddy Bear" Summer

To my little buddy,

From your big buddy,

Teddy Bear Backpack Buddy

June Theme: Teddy Bears

Backpack Buddy: small tan teddy bear

Storybook: *Golden Bear* by Ruth Young (Viking Children's Books, 1992)

Supplies:
- journal
- Letter from Teddy Bear Backpack Buddy (page 297)
- Journal Assignment, one per student (page 298)
- backpack
- Teddy Bear Backpack Buddy

Instructions:

You may wish to make the writing journals from portfolios with fasteners. Be sure there are enough journal pages (copies of page 298) for every student in the classroom to complete the writing assignment. Also place a copy of the Letter from Teddy Bear Backpack Buddy inside the journal. The homework assignment is described for parents and students in this letter. However, you may prefer to explain the assignment to students before they take it home.

For this journal assignment, students read the book *Golden Bear* and discuss the wonderful things the little boy does with his golden teddy bear. Then children pretend they go on a fun vacation with the little backpack bear. Youngsters write down where they go on the vacation and describe some of their adventures. Then they draw a picture to show some of the interesting things they did with the little backpack bear while on vacation.

Before sending the backpack home with a different child each day, check to be sure it has the small tan teddy bear, the book *Golden Bear,* and the writing journal. Remind the student who is taking these materials home to return the backpack and its contents the next school day. When it is the next school day, allow time for the student who took the backpack home to share his/her journal writing assignment with the class.

Be sure every student has an opportunity to take the backpack home. After all students have completed the writing assignment, make the journal a permanent addition to your classroom library.

Backpack Buddy

Hi!

I'm the little golden teddy bear from the storybook called *Golden Bear.* This book is in the backpack so you and your parents can read it together. I hope you like it. In the story *Golden Bear,* the little boy and I do many fun things together. After you read the book, tell your parents some of the things that the little boy and I do together.

Then pretend that you took me, your golden bear, on a vacation with you. Where did we go? How did we get there? What happened while we were on our vacation? Please use a page in this journal to tell about our vacation. Also, be sure to draw a picture to show some of the interesting things we did together.

Please don't forget to put the book *Golden Bear,* this journal, and me inside the backpack and return all these things to your teacher. You will get to share your journal assignment, and another student will get to take me home.

Bye!

Your buddy,

Little Golden Teddy Bear

Journal Assignment

Name: _____ Date: _____

Golden Bear and I decided to go somewhere very special for our summer vacation — somewhere he'd never been before; somewhere children love to go; somewhere bears only dream about. The place Golden Bear and I went to was

_____ .

We traveled by _____

and it took us _____ days to get there.

While on our vacation, a funny thing happened. Let me tell you about it.

_____

_____

_____

Here are some of the other things that happened while we were on this fun-filled vacation:

_____

_____

_____

_____

Here is a picture of some of the interesting things we did together.

Art & Poetry Activities

Dear Teddy

Supplies:

- Steps for Drawing a Teddy Bear, one per student (page 301)
- black markers, one per student
- white construction paper, one piece per student
- crayons
- "Dear Teddy" poem and "June" title, one per student (top half of page 300)
- scissors
- large piece of construction paper, any bright color; one per student
- glue
- full-body photograph of each student
- Favorite Memories, one per student (page 37)

Instructions:

Distribute the above materials to students. Discuss with students the step-by-step method of drawing a teddy bear (page 301). Have students draw a bear on the white construction paper using a black marker. Tell youngsters to color the bear. Read aloud the poem "Dear Teddy." Tell students to cut out their bear drawings, the poem, and the "June" title. Ask youngsters to glue the drawings, poem, title, and photograph of themselves onto a large piece of construction paper. Help students complete the Favorite Memories activity sheet. Then have students glue it onto the back of the large piece of construction paper.

Real Bears

Supplies:

- books with pictures of real bears
- white construction paper, one piece per student
- black markers, one per student
- crayons or markers
- glue
- "Real Bears" poem and "June" title, one per student (bottom half of page 300)
- photograph of each student (optional)
- large piece black construction paper, one per student
- Favorite Memories, one per student (page 37)

Instructions:

Show students pictures of real bears. See the bibliography (page 279) for suggestions. Distribute the other materials listed above to students. Have students use the black markers to draw outline pictures on the white construction paper of a real mother bear with her cubs inside a cave. Ask children to use the crayons or markers to color their pictures. Read aloud the poem "Real Bears" to students. Tell students to cut out the poem and the "June" title. Ask youngsters to glue the poem, title, bear cave pictures, and photograph of themselves onto a large piece of black construction paper. If students have not already done a Favorite Memories activity sheet, help them complete one now. Tell them to glue it onto the back of the black construction paper.

June Poems

Dear Teddy

Dear little teddy bear, you're such a special friend.

I know you'll be my buddy until the very end.

You're the one I tell my secrets to—

I know I can always count on you!

So let's go play and have some fun

In the cozy, warm summer sun!

June

Real Bears

A real bear isn't stuffed with fluff and it has no bows.

A real bear has claws and fur and a big wet nose.

A real bear can swim and hunt and climb.

A real bear doesn't give hugs at bedtime.

A real bear roams free and sleeps in a tree—

But I get to take my teddy bear to bed with me!

June

Steps for Drawing a Teddy Bear

Step 1

Step 2

Step 3

Step 4

Thematic Pins & Magnets

The unit about teddy bears and real bears has several cute bear patterns (below and on page 303) to accompany it. The directions for a special felt teddy bear pin/magnet are given below. These bear pins/magnets make inexpensive graduation presents at the end of a school year. There is also a graduation bear wearing a cap and gown and holding a diploma on page 303. This takes more time to make but is a wonderful reward at the end of any unit or school year.

Instructions for the pin/magnet with the bear wearing a bow tie are given below. Additional directions, as well as other ideas for materials to use when creating these gifts, are provided on page 9 of the How to Use Thematic Teaching Ideas section of this book.

Supplies:

- bear wearing a bow tie pattern (below)
- gold and red liquid embroidery paint
- white tacky glue
- stiff brown felt
- plastic eyes, two per pattern
- pin or magnetic strip, one per pattern
- scissors

Instructions:

1. Have students trace the bear pattern onto the brown felt.
2. Help students cut out the brown felt bear.
3. Tell youngsters to use the gold liquid embroidery paint to draw the bear's ears, paws, nose, and whiskers.
4. Have students use the red liquid embroidery paint to draw the bear's mouth and bow tie.
5. Ask children to glue two plastic eyes on the brown felt bear's face.
6. Help students glue a pin or magnetic strip onto the back of their felt bears.

June Patterns

End-of-Year Videotaping Ideas

The general directions for how to make a Class Video Book are on page 10 of the How to Use Thematic Teaching Ideas section of this book.

This is the last videotaping segment. Make it at least three weeks before school ends. This gives you plenty of time to make minor edits and reproduce copies, as well as for parents to order a copy of the Class Video Book.

To end the Class Video Book, it is fun to interview students, one at a time, asking them what they want to be when they grow up. After interviewing every student, have children say, *Good-bye, Mom and Dad. From* (teacher's name) _____ (grade level) *class for the* _____ *school year!"*

When the master copy is ready to be reproduced, ask a local video shop owner to add the title caption, "Our Class Video Book from _____ (teacher's name) _____ (grade level) class for the _____ school year!" to the beginning of the tape. Be sure to fill in the blanks before asking the video shop owner to create the caption.

Directly after this title caption, the first segment from September begins and all segments run consecutively, straight through to June.

The cost of the Class Video Book is reasonable because very little editing is required. The Class Video Book creates a wonderful keepsake that students and their families will cherish forever.

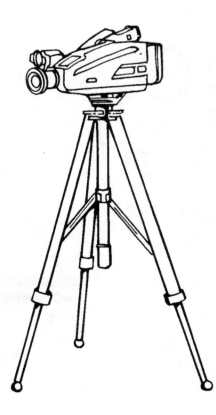